Cricket's Diary:
Our Darling Kitty

Compiled by Alice Hyman

To MY ADMIRERS

CRICKET HYMAN

VANTAGE PRESS
New York / Washington / Atlanta
Los Angeles / Chicago

To my beloved husband,
Arthur Hyman, my advisor and critic

FIRST EDITION

Copyright © 1984 by Alice Hyman

Published by Vantage Press, Inc.
516 West 34th Street, New York, New York 10001

Manufactured in the United States of America
ISBN: 533-06168-7

Library of Congress Catalog Card No.: 84-90094

All incidents attributed to Cricket are positively authentic.

All statements made by Cricket are derived from his eyes and facial expressions, but mostly from his unpredictable actions and mannerisms, and his expressive voice.

We have always said Cricket is not a cat; he is a person. As he grows older he seems to us as almost unreal. His face shows a softness and sweetness with intelligence that could only reflect pure spirit. When he looks at us—always straight in the eyes—there is a positive feeling one gets, as though his fragile spirit may suddenly fade into a mirage, leaving us with a feeling of help-lessness and vagueness. He is always obliging. When we tend or care for him, he understands and obeys without resistance, because he knows how much we love him.

The Orphanage

I was very small when my new family came to see me at the orphanage. I was in a cage with three other kitties. When they saw me I was sitting on some straw looking straight at them. My head was bent to the side. I looked like a ball of fur with two large eyes peeking out. Right then and there they said, "There he is! We want him."

They stood there close by so no one could claim me. The attendant came to look me over and said to my family, "Yes, he is a boy." She handed me over to them and I didn't cry; I let them hold me.

My mistress held me carefully. I was no bigger than her hand; she put me in a box. The attendant asked for two dollars, then off we went in a car back to our motel. My legs wobbled and bowed under me. I followed my master downstairs, but my legs were too short so I rolled down.

That night, my family put me in the bathroom to sleep. I was interested in everything, especially the water in the big white bowl. It was too high for me to climb, but one never knew what I might do. My family moved me out; surely they said I might drown, so they brought me in the living room. With each step my legs grew stronger. That night they brought me to the office, where the attendant took me in for the night.

The next morning, when my family came to pick me up, the lady said I was so full of pep she had to put me in the closet to sleep. When we left she said, "I think you will keep him; he is so cute."

Next morning we were on the way home. My master said to my mistress, "You can drive home." This surprised her because he usually does most of the driving.

I began to cry and cried almost all the way home and then fell asleep. My master didn't take his eyes off of me all the way home.

I Was Adopted

When we arrived home, my mistress carried me in a box to our neighbors, Papa Otto and Mama Pearl. I was to be a present for them. When they opened the box, they expected some fresh fruit. They looked at me and said, "No, no, we can't keep him. We do not want another kitty." I had no place to go, so my family took me home. I have a big rumpus room downstairs. There is lots of room to play and large windows to look out of. My family bought me all kinds of toys. I play with them all. I have so much fun. I love my home and my family. Soon I was hungry. I climbed on the couch, looked my mistress straight in the eyes, and said, "I am hungry." I have a pitiful cry and get impatient. Sometimes I walk on my hind legs, crying, "Hurry up!"

One morning at 6:00 A.M., my mistress opened my door and I ran under the floor. I couldn't get out and screamed with fright. My mistress pulled out a lath and I crawled through. That is how little I am. When I go outside, Papa Otto never says hello or even looks at me. Later he picked me up and smiled. Soon after he asked if the little kitten would like to play. Mama Pearl carried me back and forth in her apron. I tumbled through their garden and played in their patio. Papa Otto brought me a ball and taught me to climb a tree. I always climb down head first. Now they really love me and do not miss their kitty so much.

Angel Face

They say I have an angel face. I am just three months old. When people look at me, they say how sweet I am. But . . . when I am planning to outwit my mistress, my ears flatten and I look like mischief is coming.

I have always been very correct about my toilet. I have never made an accident. Today my mistress was coaxing me to do my duty while I sat in my box. Suddenly my ears flattened and my eyes opened wide with that special gleam of mischief. In one leap, I darted out of my box up the stairs to the breakfast room, and into my plush red basket I sat. My mistress came running after me. She picked me up and cried out, "No, no, Cricket!" It was too late. My stream was not finished and it went full into her face.

I Was Hungry

When I was two months old, I climbed up to the couch where my mistress was sitting, looked her straight in the eyes, and said, "I am hungry." I have a pitiful baby cry. Of course, I had a good healthy dinner.

Lullabye

I am four months old. My master has always loved me. When he sees me he always says hello and pats me. My mistress gives me so much love; she holds me and kisses me. I follow her every-where she goes. When my master complained, my mistress told him that he should not be just the breadwinner but give me more love. Then one day, my mistress heard him in the breakfast room singing "Rock-A-Bye Baby" off key; she peeked to see. She found me lying on my back in my master's arms; he was rocking me. I just lay there and stared at him. Now we are such good friends. He loves to flea me and gives me kisses on my forehead and under the chin. Later I sat on his lap and pushed my nose against his nose; that was my kiss.

No Mischief

My mistress tied me to the leg of the breakfast table so that I could lie in my basket without getting into mischief. Then she left the room. When she returned, I was comfortable lying on top of the table and looking at her so sweetly. There was no food on the table. I didn't do anything. How could she scold me?

The Bath

I am four months old; my mistress gave me a bath. Everyone said how beautiful I looked. Afterwards, I ran outside and sat in the dry dirt and turned to see if my mistress was watching me; she was. I picked up the dirt with my paws, and threw it into the air over my head. I looked very dirty after that. I love to go outside, but everything frightens me. The least bit of noise, and I run home with all my might. Before I leave my door, I peek through the opening and look from side to side to make sure that there is nothing to frighten me. Then I walk out and carefully look some more.

The Earthquake

We were all in the den. I was sitting on the couch. The family was looking at the television when suddenly the house began to shake. Before they knew what was happening, I was under the couch. I felt the earthquake before they did.

The Bug

I was very small, about three months old. I discovered a bug behind a cabinet in the kitchen which is a few inches away from the wall. I followed it with my eyes until I couldn't see it anymore. Then I ran to the other side to catch it. The bug did not appear; he did not come out the other end. The next morning I ran to the cabinet to see if the bug was there. The bug was gone.

Came Running

One day I visited a neighbor's yard two doors away. I heard my master calling me, but I stayed to play longer. My master hit the fence with a stick and I came home running scared. My master hit the fence again to get me inside. I just looked at him—I knew who made the noise.

Play Ball

It is fun to play ball; once when my master threw it at me I caught it. The other day we were playing ball—I chased it up and down our yard. When my master threw the ball near my door, I ran up to it and raced off in another direction. I was not going through my door into the house. I knew what they were up to.

The Curlers

I'm so curious. My mistress was sitting in her chair when I climbed on her lap to visit with her. I noticed something was different. Staring at her, I had to investigate, so I reached up to see what it was. I sniffed at them. They were curlers in her hair.

Mama Vi

I was only a few months old when I first went to visit Mama Vi. She thought I was so cute. I curled up on her neck and we both went to sleep. On my next visit, I had grown to about three months. I played at her feet and was never quiet for a moment. I crawled up on her satin couch to look at a hanging picture of some people. I stared at the large figures. That night I slept in her bed, but was not so quiet.

At six months, I came to Mama Vi's with abundant energy. I looked at her beautiful pictures hanging over the couch again.

Then I raced to the dining room and stood on the table to look at another hanging picture. I stared at it. Then I jumped down to the potted plants and dug in them. The dirt fell over the rug. Mama Vi did not say anything. My master asked her if we should give her Mama Pearl's telephone. She said, "Never mind, I'll take care of Cricket."

Well, after my family left, I had a bang-up good time. Mama Vi took me to bed with her and I made bread on her beautiful blanket. Then I ran to play on the curtains and back to jump on Mama Vi's neck and bit her. The next morning, Mama Vi was tired; she didn't sleep well that night. That day, she was up and down with me and had to run all over the house to catch me. The only time she could rest was when I got sleepy. Later in the day, she lost me and looked all over the house for me. She searched the basement and even the backyard, calling "Cricket" over and over, but I didn't answer her. Finally Mama Vi looked for me again in the kitchen, and there I was under the stove. The next evening, that is where I slept all night. After that time I never saw Mama Vi again.

Always Hungry

When I get up in the morning I am starved. When I hear my mistress upstairs, the sound of her footsteps in the kitchen, I start screaming for my breakfast regardless of what time it is in the morning. She doesn't always give me my food in the same place. Sometimes in the kitchen or in the bathroom while she is bathing. This morning I was so excited. I ran asking, "Where? Where?" I could not see the dish right in front of me. She had to put it under my nose before I knew it was there. Afterwards I said, "Thank you." I am not usually so polite.

The Chair Rungs,
the Table and the Glass

When my family first brought me home, they visited some

friends. I was tiny and full of pep. The first thing I did was run to the dining-room table with six chairs. When I got to the chair, I jumped over each rung, then went on to all the other chairs and returned to where I had started. Now today my family was preparing the table for six guests. I jumped on the table and walked straight through, looking all the way from side to side, stopping at each glass until I reached the other side.

Eating

I am five months old now. When I was very small, my mistress had to spoon-feed me. Later she broke up the food and put it in my mouth. I ate delicately. Now I run to my dish and gobble the food. Sometimes I look up at my mistress to say it is so good. Then I ask for my dessert, which is brewer's yeast, carrot, juice, and vitamins. After all that, I burp. When it's all finished, I purr and climb up on her lap. I put my two paws on her shoulders and press my nose against hers so hard her head falls back. This tells her that I love her.

The Door

Papa Otto taught me how to open the door when I was a tiny kitten. Now, I know which door opens away and which one opens toward me. The hall door leading to the kitchen opens toward me. I learned to put my paw through the opening if it is not closed and pull the door open. This morning my mistress was in the breakfast room. She heard a mysterious creaking sound and got up to investigate. She saw my paw in the door when I was trying to open it. I turned quickly to run from her, but she chased me down the hall to the den door; it opens away. I got to the door as my mistress was closing it. I hit my head not very hard, but it hurt. I shook it several times. My mistress saw that I was disappointed, so she picked me up to comfort me. This time I lost, but I never give up.

I Am Called Cricket

I am called Cricket because when I was a tiny kitten, I was quick and cute. Also, my face is very expressive—so people say. When I get mischievous, I roll my eyes, flatten my ears, and think, "Shall I or shall I not; I guess I will." Then I pounce on my mistress; I have very strong baby teeth, but I don't mean to hurt her.

I am considered beautiful, but not as a purebred. I am part Persian, with long gray fur. When I walk, I swish my behind like an elegant lady. My tail is gorgeous!

I am curious about everything and I love to taste things. One day I played with a string; it got shorter and shorter. Then my mistress caught me and pulled and pulled on the string; about eight inches came out.

Today we went to the veterinarian. I had on my harness and I looked elegant as usual. I stalked into the room where others were waiting. I walked to a rubber tree and sat in the box; the tree was too small to climb. I visited with everybody. All the animals were so well behaved. The people laughed when I hissed at three cats in their cages. They thought that I have a very high IQ and behaved most unusually. Then we saw the doctor. She picked me up, kissed me, and said, "Look at that baby face; you give your mother so much worry!"

I Help Myself

I am now six months old. I always love to eat. I am in the kitchen just as soon as I hear footsteps there. The food is served to me carefully and is nourishing. I get so anxious before it is ready. When my mistress serves me, she puts on my dinner jacket, which is a red harness, then she makes me perform. Well, I've gotten so good that I sit up automatically for it. But now, don't you think that is asking too much of me just to get my dinner? I do, and believe me, when it isn't enough, I wait until she is not looking and help myself if I can find some goodies. My family can't watch me all the time. This morning, I had a slice of butter from the table.

Yesterday I nibbled on some leftovers in the sink. When my mistress is in the breakfast room, she can't see me, so I look for treats. When I hear her move the chair, I know she knows, so I jump off the sink with my head bowed down, but only for a moment. Then I help myself to anything more that looks good, if I can find it.

A Big Bite

My mistress often surprises me with a special treat for dinner. This time it was so good that I couldn't wait to get it all down. So I grabbed another big mouthful. It was too large to chew or swallow, so when she asked how I liked it, I tried to answer her without dropping it. My mistress laughed because this was too much to believe. I said, "Wow!"

Ten Ju

Uncle John, our medical friend, came to dinner last night. The conversation is often regarding his kitty, Ten Ju, and me. I have a flea collar on, since it is flea time, but Ten Ju is allergic to it so Uncle John has to bathe her. This time he left her standing for a long time with some medication on her. She was very wet because he was trying to kill all the fleas. She didn't complain at all that time, but as he picked her up to dry her, she sank her teeth into his arm. Lucky for him he had his coat on.

Jealousy

My mistress was downstairs in the laundry room when I flashed through my door and up the stairs. She saw a little maltese cat follow me, growling all the way. I waited in the hall, trembling with rage and jealousy while she showed him to my master. She picked me up to love me, but I was not agreeable. Instead, I hissed, screamed, and growled; then I tore away from her arms. I thought my mistress had forsaken me. Of course, my family was shocked. How could I behave like that? My mistress put me in my room to calm down. All day I refused to speak to her, and even refused my dessert. Later she had to spoon-feed me. I lay on the chair while she opened my mouth to swallow; I finished it all. Next morning, we were good friends. Later my mistress spoke to the kitty's family; she learned that his name is Mew.

A Bad Taste

My mistress put me outside this morning. After about half an hour, I was sitting on the wet lawn, staring in our window. Later she came out to bring me inside. I growled as she wiped off my feet. She scolded me, then she noticed that I was licking my mouth and making a most unusual noise. It sounded slushy and hollow. When she reached for the telephone to call emergency hospital, she noticed the foam on my face as I opened my mouth to get rid of whatever was in it. My master said, "Oh-oh, he's been trying to eat a garden snail." The family was grateful that there was no catastrophe. Later my mistress put me on the bed with my master. They couldn't believe that I stayed there with him because every morning we go through the usual routine—my love for the kitchen and what's in it. This time I stayed with my master; he had a bad cold. Then I gave him a great big kiss on his nose. I didn't leave until my mistress came to get me.

Mew

Lately my mistress has been noticing that my personality is changing. I get annoyed if I am held when I want to get down. I tell her so and this is so unusual, because I am really very sweet. My mistress began to see the reason for my changed disposition.

She remembered talking with Love's master, who said she was getting very mean. Now he keeps her indoors; she can never go outside again. It all became quite clear to my mistress; my chum, Mew, has such a bad disposition and we both played together. Actually Mew is always growling, so I got into the habit. My mistress kept me indoors. In two days I became sweet again. My family thought it interesting that this should happen with animals, as well as people.

Out of My Harness

We had company for the weekend. They were impressed with my soft manner. I did my routing for them, which made them laugh. Afterwards my mistress tied me outside in the sunshine. Then Mama Pearl called to tell my family that I was no longer there. My leash was hanging on the fence and I had taken off with my friend Pasha. It is a beautiful day. I have no intention of going home unless I get hungry.

My Door

We got up at six in the morning. My mistress gave me breakfast and weighed me. Afterwards, I wanted outside as usual; my door was opened and out I flashed. Later she came out to call me. The first time no answer, the second time no answer. The third time, I ran out from Papa Otto's yard, yawning. She coaxed me, but I had no intention of coming in. My mistress closed my door. She waited for half an hour. Sure enough, when she returned, I was at my door, waiting and waiting. I am still very young. I get quite concerned if I am left alone outside. My master came to watch me. I cried. They waited fifteen minutes before the door was opened. I flew inside and upstairs. The family followed me. Where do you think I went? Of course, upstairs into the kitchen. I was promised dinner the first time and I expected it.

New Harness

The family decided I must be dressed up when we go shopping, so we went to the pet shop for a new harness. I was so glad to be in the car that I purred and kissed the family. I was going with them. When we got there, my mistress put me on my back to fit the harness. The storeman was surprised that I behaved so gently. He kept saying to my mistress, "I can't get over him. He is so sweet." He smiled and smiled. Then he petted me.

The Tree

It was five o'clock in the evening during winter. I was outside enjoying Papa Otto's garden. My special door was closed and no one was around. Later it grew darker—too dark to see anything. My family called and called. When I didn't answer, they were worried that someone had stolen me. Finally Papa Otto turned on the searchlight. He flashed it on the tree, and there I was, high up in the branches. They were so happy to see me. I didn't say anything; I just observed them. Then I came down the tree head first to the ten foot ladder, and walked down. Everyone knew that I enjoyed all the commotion. My mistress said, "Oh, dear, Cricket. You are such a problem kitty."

The Operation

I became eight months old, so my family left me in the hospital for my special operation. I was to stay overnight, but that afternoon the doctor said I was so healthy that I could go home. When my family came to pick me up, I looked at them. I tried to tell them all about myself, but in the middle of the story, my eyes closed. I yawned and yawned until bedtime and then fell asleep.

The Family Came Home

Today my family came home. My mistress called me from the door. I was two lots away when she called. I ran as fast as I could to see her. When I got to the fence, I was so excited that I fell off and had to make another jump. Of course, I got all kinds of love and kisses. Now my mistress is in her chair, writing all about me, and I am on her lap. I gave her so many kisses on her nose that she finally had to put me on a chair next to her, but that is not enough. I am back on her lap, purring, kneading with my paws. I insist on staying on her lap; it is difficult for her to write. I won't leave her alone. I am still a teenager and behave like one, but tonight it is different. I am so happy to have my family back, and I want to be near them. Later I gave my master kisses too as he went back and forth with the luggage. Then he picked me up and hugged me. I was so happy I purred and purred. For three days, I stayed close to home. I left for a little while, then came back to be sure my family did not leave me again. Soon my mistress called me a monster.

The next day I went out at 8:00 A.M.; it was a beautiful day. My mistress called me several times, but I would not come in. She decided to teach me a lesson. She locked my special door that swings both ways. When she returned an hour later, my nose was right at my door, my tail wagging back and forth. She pulled the shades down with just enough opening to peek through, and rapped on the door window. I heard her and saw that my door was still closed. This time I was worried; I stared at it and looked back and forth, first to Papa Otto's yard and then to my door. I ran to the fence that runs along the side of the house near a window. My mistress thought that I had jumped over the fence, but I was trying to peek under the window shade to see her. She opened the shade and there I was, inside the iron bars of the window. Of course, my door was opened for me. I ran through it. I allowed her to pick me up. She kissed me and forgave me.

The Accident

Today my mistress had to go to a friend's home on an emergency. She put my harness on and off we went in our two-door Pinto. When we arrived at the friend's home, my mistress forgot all about me. A few hours later, she returned to the car and drove off, thinking about the serious emergency. A few blocks later, she called me and I didn't answer. She turned the car around so fast and drove back. She found part of my leash at the home of her friend and my harness with the rest of the leash one and a half blocks away. She called and called me. Some men were working on the street with an automatic hammer. The noise was awful, more than I ever heard. I was frozen with fear. Soon I could hear my mistress and kept answering her. When she found me, I was on someone's front porch hiding behind a potted tree. She picked me up and put me in the car, then she felt me all over for injuries. No one really knows what happened, but they think I got out of the car when my mistress returned; she drove off without checking me.

I hung by my harness, dragging my feet. Then I must have pulled out of my harness. My paws were raw. Lucky for me Uncle John, the doctor, came to dinner. He said to me, "That will teach you a lesson." He watched me as I lay on the chair, and said I would heal my feet by licking them. The next day we all went to my doctor. He took my face and hugged me, then he called me a dear.

He said I had colitis. I was in shock for three days and had to be carried around.

7:00 A.M. Observer

It was seven in the morning, and we were all in the gym. Suddenly I jumped off the chair. I saw something and looked all around the room. It was an insect flying. I called out, "Look, look!" and chased it until it disappeared. I shared this experience with the family and they understood.

14

A Bit of Pork

My mistress decided to give me a small bit of pork this morning with my oatmeal mush. I started to eat and was so surprised. I looked up at her and said, "It's good."

Yeast Carrot Juice

Today I decided that I don't like yeast with spinach, celery, and carrot juice, which my mistress gives me every day. I refused it again, so when my mistress came after me with the spoon, I ran to the chair where she has to spoon-feed me. It is amazing how I oblige her when she puts the spoon in my mouth. Maybe it doesn't taste so bad because I let her do it, and I swallow the stuff.

Baby Pasha

The most unusual little kitty came by while I was in my play-yard. He is all black except for a white streak under his chin and neck. He has white paws. He looks like a baby devil. He cries so funny; no one has ever heard such a strange baby cry. He is about four months old. He has small eyes. My mistress, of course, was delighted with him. She picked him up and loved him for a long time. After that, we did not see him for about three months.

Really, you can't imagine how he has changed. His family moved away and gave him to their neighbor three doors away. His name is Pasha; my mistress can't get near him, he is so mean. He still has that most unusual baby cry; it is really funny the family loves to hear him. They are anxious to make friends with him, but he is so mean they can't pick him up. He growls and screams. His new family gives him the best there is, yet he is the meanest kitty there is.

Of course, my mistress won't give up. Now when he comes in our house to visit, he gets a snack, then runs after me and I get clobbered. The worst of it is that he has his claws out, which makes me cry out. The family thinks Pasha is angry because his first family left him when he was a baby.

Best Treat

Today was the best treat of all. I waited until my mistress left the kitchen, then I looked for goodies. I found my master's cup with the brewer's yeast he forgot to eat. When my mistress came back, the cup was on the floor and I was eating as fast as I could because I heard her coming. I looked so happy that my mistress could not scold me. She laughed and kissed me. The yeast was still on my chin when she put me down.

Little Sophisticate

Today I surprised my family. They had to go downtown on an errand, so they took me with them in the car. I had on my harness. They had to walk two blocks to the office, so they decided to carry me there. They were surprised that I was not afraid. The men were working in the street with trip hammers. Trucks were passing by, making more noise, but I just took it all calmly. I looked around and watched everything as we passed by. When we got to the office, the secretary stopped her work to talk to me. She brought out some rubber bands for me to play with, but I was not in a playful mood. I did behave nicely. She told us all about her kitty; how much fun they have. We were there for a half hour, then the boss came out. He also talked to me. He remarked to the family that I look and behave in a regal way. The family was proud that I was finally learning to enjoy people more and more.

Gourmet

My mistress calls me a gourmet kitty. Just now I ate canned cat food, cottage cheese, and cooked peas. I always eat what she gives me, except for a time when my chum, the maltese kitty, would invite me over to share his pot-luck dinners. My mistress grew suspicious because I did not lick my dish clean, or ask for dessert, and refused some dry snacks. I was growing big around my tummy, so my mistress began to weigh me; each day I grew fatter. She talked it over with my chum's family, so now they keep his food inside. I'm back to eight and a half pounds and feel much peppier now.

Stopper

I love my mistress so much that I want to chew her up, and that's what I have been doing. By now her hands have bites and scratches on them. My mistress does not appreciate my love. I just won't stop, so today she took my paw and pinched it. I cried, then bit her again, just because I want to win. Well, now when I begin to chew on her, she reminds me and I remember. So I just bite a teeny bit to show my love.

Fun Day

Today was one of my most fun days. The family cleared the dishes and put the kitchen in order, then left the room for the den. Soon they heard a loud crash. The family came running. On the table my mistress had left a glass of milk. It was turned over, with broken pieces of glass on the table and more glass on the floor. I was drinking the milk. They were afraid a small piece could be in the glass and also some on the floor with the spilled milk. Surely I must have cut myself or swallowed some glass. My master solved the problem. He put all the pieces together. All but one piece completed the glass. My mistress was so frightened, she threw the last piece in the garbage by mistake, but she found it later. The family was so upset that they forgot to scold me. Soon the house was peaceful again. Ten minutes later, there came another crash. This time they found me on the table, looking at another shattered glass I had thrown on the floor. There was no more milk to drink, no reason for such naughtiness; I just wanted to get some more attention.

Pasha's Winning Ways

My mistress looked out the window to check on me. I was out in my usual place, where there is a box and a sack for me. She saw Pasha sitting in my box, and I was sitting on the sack. Soon after, Pasha was on my sack, and I was sitting on the dirt.

Am I Stubborn!

I guess I must give my family a bad time, but after all, I have my moods and sometimes I just don't want to do everything every day the same way.

Besides, all that hassle over my personal manners I was really following along quite regularly. Now, for the last three days, I positively refuse to perform in my room. So yesterday my master took me outside and coaxed me with "Good boy, hurry up, quickly," and all the other magic words. Well, all I did was smell the flowers and eat the green grass. Next day they kept me all day in my room. By the evening there was nothing, so my master took me out once more and all went well. They wonder about me. Why am I so stubborn? Well, it is great to see them get so upset once in a while.

My Master

My master loves me very much. I love him too, because when he fleas me, I purr and close my eyes. Afterwards, my master rocks me and I fall asleep. When he is looking at the T.V., he usually says to my mistress, "Don't talk to me; I want to look at the picture!" Last night when I got on his lap, he did not look at the picture; instead he petted me for one hour. I lay there so contented. Not every kitty has such a loving master.

Usual Appetite

Today I went into the kitchen with my usual appetite. I ate some food from my bowl, then looked at my mistress and sniffed at my usual oatmeal, with milk and all her goodies, which I usually eat because I am so hungry. This time, I said no to her; then she asked me why. I sniffed at it and said no again, quietly. Now she was worried about me. She picked me up, brought me and my dish to my room, and said, "You are not going to bully me," then closed the door. When she returned ten minutes later, my dish was empty. I couldn't convince her; she is wising up to me.

The Hose

Today I ran to Papa Otto's yard and climbed up the tree. Papa Otto was not home. Soon the family began to call. When I didn't come in, they looked and saw me in the branches. I wouldn't come down, so my master gave me a shot of water with the hose. I ran to the fence and sat down. My master gave me another squirt. I jumped into the next yard and hid under a plant. My master saw me, so I got another squirt. Then I jumped down and went to my door. The last squirt brought me to Papa Otto, who picked me up. My master just didn't know how to handle me.

Vitamin C

My mistress prepared my dinner, which is always delicious. I usually pounce on it and it is gone in a few minutes. This time my mistress had to prepare 500 mg of vitamin C. She crushed it and added a little water, then poured it over my food as I was eating. I stopped, looked at it and at her, then walked out of the kitchen. My mistress was ashamed. She said, "Oh, Cricket, I am sorry." Then she put out a new dinner for me. I came back and ate it.

I Adore My Master

During the summer I am affected by many fleas. I scratch and scratch, so my master decided to comb me more often. Twice a day he combs me carefully. I am so grateful that I purr all the while. He talks to me as I turn my head to show him where the fleas are. Before we were good friends; now I adore him. I also put my two paws on his shoulders and kiss him hard on his nose. He loves me to sit on his lap and I would stay longer, except that I want to see what is going on in the kitchen. So I jump off and make a running leap in the air. Off I go. The fleas can stay a little while longer. In the kitchen I might get a smidgen of something good from my mistress—especially if I insist.

Bedtime

After my mistress put me to bed, I heard her coming downstairs again. I called her and she opened the door. I was sitting in my proper place and looking at her while I performed. My mistress said, "Good boy," and patted me as I sat there. Then I shook my front paws off and hopped out. It is nice to have the family say good night to me.

Our Agreement

My mistress and I have a special agreement. You remember I told you how my mistress hides all those things she calls goodies in my oatmeal mush. When she gives me my breakfast, she pours half and half over the oatmeal to disguise it. So now I drink the cream and tell her I want more. That's our agreement, so she pours more over it—anything to get it down my throat. Of course, before you know it, I have had a half-cup of cream, which is too much. Today when she weighed me, the scale was alarming, so her plan is not working.

Well, this morning I went back and forth saying, "I want more cream." She understood perfectly, but now she has another plan and it will work. She will spoon-feed me that stuff in a teaspoon, then I can enjoy the real flavor of oatmeal mush. All went well, but now my mistress has decided that I must learn to eat what is put before me. Today I got so much milk with my oatmeal. She wonders how I get all the icky stuff down.

I Always Win

I have a special door to go in and out, and I guard it. When my mistress comes I run outside before she can close my door. When we are upstairs I know what she is going to do, so we race downstairs. I always win!

Too Late

We get up early in the morning, sometimes about six o'clock. This morning, after my breakfast of oatmeal and kidney platter with milk, I was still hungry. I opened the door under the sink and said something to myself. Then I came out with my goodies and ate them. I had some left-over sardines that I found in the garbage can. No one saw me until it was too late.

Race

We had a race again. My mistress got to the door first and banged it closed. I came between it and the door jamb, hitting my head very hard. My mistress put an ice pack on each side as I lay there with my eyes closed. The family was worried, but I was only enjoying the ice packs and attention. Soon I jumped off her lap and began to wash myself.

Tiger

I have a new friend and he lives in the same house that Mew did. I enjoy good company; often he comes calling me in a loud voice. When the family looks out to see, he disappears. He fights with another kitty in the middle of the night, right under our window. My mistress became suspicious because my scale showed a half-pound gain in weight. She checked with Tiger's mistress and it seems that I have been sharing Tiger's food. One day I was with my friend and didn't come in for dinner—the first time since she had been calling me. I returned only after I was ready to come home. Today she called for a long time so I started to run home. When I got to the fence, Tiger screamed, "Don't go!" So I turned to look at him and ran back.

Papa Otto

It was a cold, foggy day, but I still wanted out, so the door was opened for me. When my mistress came to get me two hours later, I was in Papa Otto's yard. He was not there. She called, "Dinner!" and I looked at her, then to Papa Otto's door four times. I absolutely refused to come, even for a ride. So my mistress gave up and left me. On thinking it over, my mistress began to understand; I was trying to tell her that I wanted to play with Papa Otto. For the first time I could make her understand.

Painting the Fence

My master was painting the fence; it is a beautiful green. I went out to watch him; he said a few words to me, then he forgot about me. When my mistress came outside to see my master, he said, "Oh, Cricket just walked on the fence." My mistress was horrified. She caught me up in her arms to see. She saw my feet were covered with paint. By that time they were both concerned. My mistress cleaned my front paws with cleaning fluid. I screamed

22

with pain and began to lick my paws. She quickly washed my feet with soap and water, but I still cried. She called the doctor, who was worried that I could be very ill. He told them to watch for certain signs. Licking the cleaning fluid from my feet and smelling the fumes could cause severe illness. They were told to rush me to the hospital if symptoms appeared. My family was so grateful that nothing happened. They held me in their arms for a long time. The next day I was fine.

Little Charmer

The family resolved when I was very small never to spoil me, so they never feed me at the table. At that time I didn't know very much—I was only two months old. All the goodies were on the table ready to eat and I didn't even see them. I would play at their feet, entertain them, and kept them laughing. They often remark how I show my love for them. Now the family questions my intentions—"Food?" This morning, my mistress was eating her breakfast; I had a large meal and ate enough for my size. I sat on a chair in front of her. All she could see were my magnetic eyes. She thought I looked so sweet and innocent; but could I be scheming? Then I came to her side, purring and pushing my face into her hand. This will usually go on for quite a while as long as she sits there eating. Many times she will refuse me if I am overweight. This time she caught me in her arms (I let her catch me), and gave me a little leftover. Again, I charmed her; she gave in to me.

Hangover

This morning I have a hangover. That is what my master told me. Yesterday my mistress prepared the biscuits for baking. When she returned, I was eating a whole raw biscuit. The family was quite concerned, so they called my doctor, who said to give me a physic. Of course, right afterward I didn't feel so good, so I went downstairs to lay on my master's robe, which was on the washing machine.

I Told Her

I love my mistress so much and I like to show her. Today we were in the yard. I suddenly jumped on her with all my might. I grabbed her ankle and kicked her with my hind feet as hard as I could. She said, "No, no, Cricket," and pushed me away. With that I went to a sack on the ground. I grabbed it, kicked as hard as I could with my hind feet, and stared at her. I showed her that I could still do it.

Tiger

The family heard Tiger screaming in the garage. They ran to see what it was all about. It was Tiger talking to me. My mistress picked me up. I snarled and growled, not at her but at Tiger. I did not want her to be near him. So I jumped out of her arms and ran outside. Tiger came running after me.

Tiger and I

Here I am, 7:00 A.M., sitting on Papa Otto's platform that he built. I am tied with a leash long enough to walk around a little. I am happy and don't mind it at all. My mistress says that children like to be disciplined; so I guess little kitties like it too. I can see all around and hear the birds singing. Just now my master came out to see how I was doing; he found Tiger sitting next to me. Tiger jumped down and stared at my master. I enjoyed my morning outing. Papa Otto came out with some fish bits and petted me.

Next morning I was angry with my mistress. It was cold outside and she tied me up again. I was upset and told her so. I had a box with a warm rug to sit in, so she did not worry. When the sun began to shine, she moved me there; I had more room to play. I was happy.

When my mistress returned soon after, she found the rope twisted around the petunias and my leash hanging there. She was annoyed but I wasn't. Three hours later, she saw me. I returned to play in my yard.

The Orphan

After Mew moved away, another kitty came to our neighborhood. He looks like me, except he has short fur and black stripes. My family says he has feet like the sphinx. His eyes are large and look so sad. I talked with him as we sat on the fence. He was frightened of everyone and looked starved. Every day the orphan got thinner. His ribs hung out. Finally he came to beg for food. He was polite to my family, but when he came through my door one day, he hissed at me. I became afraid of him.

My family kept me in my room. One morning my master went to the basement and the little orphan came through my door, crying. My master shooed him away but he cried so pitiously for food that the family began to hurt for him; he looked like a shadow. They couldn't stand it any longer. My mistress ran upstairs to get some milk for him. He drank and drank. Then he ate some canned food. It looked like he would never have enough. The family was sad to see such hunger.

He was still hungry when he left the house. Next morning Orphan was waiting for us. My mistress kept filling his dish. When he was finished, my mistress picked him up. He seemed afraid at first, then he looked at her with his big, green eyes. He seemed to be smiling at her and began to purr. My mistress held him longer while she petted him; he loved it.

By now the family was attached to him—his sweet, smiling face always thanking them. How could they abandon him? They loved him now.

They called the SPCA, who reported that if he was not adopted in three days, he would be put to sleep.

By now the family was concerned. He looked so pitiful, thin and scrawny, they decided to bring him to a pet shelter. My mistress put my harness and leash on him and drove off. She was surprised with his behavior. He sat quietly on her lap all the way, looking at her with that shining expression. He allowed her to carry him across the busy street with no fear—he trusted her. She held him on her lap, waiting for their appointment. Several people commented on his beauty.

The doctor examined him while my mistress watched on, and then my mistress left with a feeling of sadness. His love was overwhelming; she felt as though she had let him down.

The family never forgot the orphan. There were so many kitties there for adoption and they wondered about him. A few weeks later, they returned to visit the orphan. There were a dozen cages with homeless kitties, and a special room with toys for kittens. The family was impressed with all this care given to them all.

They found the orphan still under the effects of his operation. He lay there in his cage, sleeping. When my mistress called to him, he suddenly came to life. He recognized her; his happiness was overwhelming and painful. They left the orphan there thinking that he would still be there when they returned. However when they went to visit him again, he was gone—a lady had adopted him. The family was very disappointed, for they loved the orphan, never realizing that they would never see him again.

If my family could only see the orphan and visit with his new mistress, then I would have a little playmate.

Yesterday I heard the family discussing the little orphan who had come to our house. The family went to the adoption center to make further inquiries regarding the orphan. They were told by the attendant that the orphan had been adopted on August 3. This surprised the family, since there had been so many other kittens there, waiting for someone to love them. When they asked for the address, they were told that the new owner's name and address could not be given out. This disappointed them so much that my mistress called the doctor who examined the orphan. The doctor checked with the attendant. The attendant talked with the new owner, who inquired why the family hadn't called before and told them please not to bother her. The doctor suggested that another doctor in charge would try to convince her. My mistress thought it curious that this incident should be so closely related to a human relationship when a child is adopted. The new mother will protect her child to keep it.

My Face

So many people say that I have a very expressive face. When others talk to me, I always look at them straight in the eyes—especially when I've done something naughty, like the day we had company for lunch. While they were eating, I nipped on the pie—that time they didn't see me. Another time I jumped on the sink board and helped myself. I am embarrassed when my mistress scolds me after I have done something. I put my head down and run out. The other day I jumped on the stove to help myself. I am never given food at the dinner table. My mistress was concerned that I would get burned, but I was unconcerned about my crime. Now the kitchen is always closed—if they can remember.

Another Spanking

My family thinks that I am changing. I have my own ideas about certain things. When I wanted outside, my mistress picked me up and said, "No, Cricket, you can't go out." I was angry and spoke up; I told her so. When I wouldn't stop growling, she spanked my behind and said, "Don't you talk to me like that." Later she put my harness on and let me sit on the platform. I did enjoy that, so when she came out to see me, I told her that I wanted to stay, but did not growl. When she picked me up, I refused to go. She insisted and brought me inside. Again, they think that I am such a naughty kitty.

27

The Cat Fight

We were all sitting in the den. There was a loud screaming. I looked out of the window and saw Tiger glaring at Long Tail. He is cream with a long, dark tail. They were going at it. I got so excited; I ran to the door to get out so I could see the fight. My mistress picked me up and said, "No!" I returned to the window and watched it. It was getting louder and louder. I got more excited. My mistress pulled me back again.

Bird Bath

I adore Papa Otto's garden. When the wind blows, everything moves. It is so exciting, I don't know which leaf or bug to catch, so I leap frontward and backward, to the left and to the right, turning somersaults in the air and on the ground. The birdbath is the most exciting. It is always full of water. I jump on the bath to see what is in it. Papa Otto shakes his head. He is upset. The birdbath is for little birds who want to bathe. Now I am enjoying it so much that it is getting a little wobbly from my acrobatics. Worst of all, there are the little birds who come every day to drink and bathe. I can't keep away. Papa Otto put some mesh screen on the sides and sticks to hold it, but this, of course, makes it easier for me to climb on it. One time my mistress came to my room. I was playing with a poor little dead bird; some naughty kitty did it. My mistress was heartsick. She had to bury it with sadness. Now the birds don't come so often to bathe, but I have a new plan. When my mistress comes about, looking and calling me, I never answer her. She knows why; she sees me lying under a large plant near the birdbath. I just lie there looking at her. My mistress had her plan. She opened the hose spray full force on me. I jumped out running and looked up in the sky, thinking it must be raining. In a few seconds, I was through my door and home.

Breakfast

The family has been home for two days now. As usual, I met them at the door with lots of affection. I smiled and stayed around them all day.

This morning, my mistress came downstairs to give me breakfast. I was so glad to see her and turned to see if she was coming with me. She wasn't. For the first time, she had decided to do some chores, and forgot about me. A few minutes later, I came back to her and said, "Please come with me." Of course she did. I hadn't touched my breakfast yet, but when she walked into the kitchen, I was waiting for her and began to eat. Then, as usual, I looked up at her and smiled because it is so good.

Autumn Bath

It has been so hot when I go outside that the earth is dusty. So my mistress gives me the usual sponge bath. She rubs my fur with a wet rag. Usually the rag is very dirty. That's what I get on her when she picks me up. It means a sponge bath every day. Today was worse; my master caught twenty fleas altogether on me. My mistress decided to give me a real bath. I complained. Later she thought she would tie me to a long leash in Papa Otto's yard. I didn't mind, but my leash was not long enough. So I pulled and pulled. When she came out to see if I was okay, I was gone two lots away. I won again. I didn't even try to answer her call. I just walked farther away.

What Is a Kitty To Do?

You know how tricky my mistress can be. I never know what she is going to do to me. When I am in the kitchen, they have to be alert because I never miss an opportunity if I see food around. But the kitchen isn't always the safest place to stay. Usually that is where she gets to me. Just when I am sitting there quietly, she comes up to me with some excuse or other. So today I knew she was up to something. But what else is a kitty to do? So I just let her do it and she did. She poured something in a teaspoon and then she gave it to me. Boy, was I surprised! It didn't taste bad, and, in fact, it was good!

Pasha and the Yard

My master put me in my yard, tied me, and left. There was a box for me to sit in and also a sack on the lawn. My master was working in the garden. I sat in the box to watch him. My master turned to look at me and in that instant, Pasha ran toward me and turned my box over. I went with it. I looked so surprised at Pasha and got out, then I sat down on the ground. Pasha jumped in the box, looking pleased. Later, my mistress came by to talk to me. Just then, Pasha ran to me and gave me a swat in my face with his claws out. I ducked and moved away. Pasha came up to my mistress and rolled on his back, saying, "Love me, love me."

Chicken

Today my master went downstairs to find the garbage can turned over, with food scattered around. The meat paper was chewed up and goodness knows what else I found to eat. My scale shows more weight, so now that problem was solved. The garbage can is sure to be covered. Now whenever I go downstairs to see what goodies I can eat, I see the cans are closed tightly. But there is always the kitchen—I got through again when no one was looking. When my master came in here, I was gobbling a great big piece of chicken with a large bone. My master grabbed me and pulled it right out of my mouth. Now the family vows to put a lock on the door.

Health Food

You remember when I made a remark about carrots, spinach, and celery juice? At that time I was pretty up about it. You see, when my mistress calls out "Dinner!" I expect something solid, like choice bits or a treat from the refrigerator, but when she calls "Dinner!" and expects me to like carrots, spinach, and celery juice with yeast—that's a different story. I walked away with my tail up high. Finally, she understands I can enjoy that stuff when it is given to me quietly, without a great fuss about how good it is for me. Then I lap up the whole bit without any fuss. It takes time for the family to understand me and sometimes it is distressing when they don't.

Little Demon

When Pasha gets angry, he is very angry. My mistress has lots of his imprints on her hands. When she spanks him, in an instant he stops. We both understand when she spanks us. Pasha and I have our bouts. He comes up to me. We kiss and talk it over. Then the next instant he clobbers me with his right paw and I return it with my left paw (I am left-pawed). When someone is nice to Pasha, one never knows what he will do. The family says he is like a naughty boy who enjoys being naughty. He really looks so wicked with his small eyes, all-black face, and that white mask on his chin, which runs down his neck. Truly they say he is a little demon. His bad temper is catching.

Windowsill

One evening I perched myself in the windowsill in the bedroom, which rises fifteen feet above a concrete patio walk. My mistress came into the room and looked at me with a shocked expression. I dared her to catch me. This time I would win. I could jump off the windowsill. She walked around the room, ignoring me, then left me. Both she and my master were fearful that I would jump off the sill and be injured. My mistress got an idea. She went to the kitchen and called, "Dinner!" In a flash I was there. The family breathed again and closed the window.

Two Years Old

Today is my birthday. I am two years old. The family called me in for dinner. There was lamb and chicken with peas. I began to eat while they looked on. It was so good! I was really surprised, so I turned my head to look at my family. I was absolutely over-joyed! Never have they seen such an expression on my face.

Pound Cake

The day before yesterday, I opened a pound cake wrapped in cellophane and ate a big piece out of it—the size of a large slice of bread.

Yesterday I turned a glass of milk over on the table and began to drink as fast as I could until my mistress caught me. She heard the glass fall and came running.

Today my master prepared a hamburger for himself. It was ready to eat, so he put it in the cooler. Before he came back, I opened the door and pulled out the hamburger and was eating it. My mistress was doing something and didn't see me.

Every time they scold me, I bow my head in shame but I never seem to learn my lesson. Mama Pearl calls me Peck's Bad Boy. I have such a sweet, intelligent face, one would never dream that I could behave so naughty.

Tricky

A few months ago, my mistress opened the kitchen door to prepare some food for dinner. Of course, I was right behind her.

When she saw me, she stepped out of the room and quietly walked through the living room and dining room into the kitchen again. Of course, she fooled me. I heard her fussing around.

Today my master started for the kitchen only to see me right there at his heels, following him. He shut the door, then sneaked around to the dining-room door. When he opened it, I went through first; that time I fooled him!

Comfort Box

I was such a tiny kitten and most careful about my toilet. When I was two months old, my mistress brought me over to visit Mama Vi for the afternoon. Later, my mistress came to get me and put me in the car. Just as soon as we got going, I began to cry. She stopped the car and put me in my comfort box. I refused to use it. I still cried, so she had to rush a screaming kitten home. When we arrived, I went straight to my room and did what I had to do. Now I am older.

Today, we started out for shopping. Just as we got going, I informed them of my need. My mistress said, "Cricket, why didn't you think of that before we left?" She said it just as though I would understand. There was no comfort box, so they had to rush me back home.

Now there is always one in the car. I think nothing of it—just get in the comfort box and do what must be done while the car is moving.

She Can't Catch Me

I am always wary when my mistress calls me in that coy, sweet voice. There is a usual time when I am anxious to go home, but not when she calls me at any other time. Today, I did come in; I had a few bites to eat that were not appetizing, so I turned away. Then I saw her reach for me. As usual, she can never catch me. She ran to the kitchen door, but I got there first. She forgot to close the hall door, so I skipped out. She gets so exasperated because every time I turn the tables on her, I always win.

Folding Door

My mistress gets so frustrated with me. All day, as long as I am gone, my family is going into one room or another to find me. That's my best talent—hiding. Our living room is off the hall and kitchen. It is easy to slip in there when no one is watching. I enjoy the Persian rugs very much. They are soft and fun to sharpen my claws. My mistress does not approve, so my master put up a folding door to close off the living room. That put a stopper on my favorite playground. For months I was isolated. Then one morning my mistress thought she heard a strange noise coming from upstairs, so she thought and looked all over for me. I was nowhere to be found. Later she opened the folding doors. I was there in the living room. I had jumped over the folding doors. She could not imagine me jumping so high, but I proved it to her.

Indian Summer

I usually never go outside before my dinnertime, which is around two o'clock. When I have eaten, I can't wait to get out. After my dinner today, I ran out through my door. The day was warm after three weeks of fog and cold weather. It was all so great that I wouldn't come home; nothing could entice me. The family called and called me, but I never let them see me. Finally, about 5:00 P.M., Mama Pearl came to the rescue. She called me and I flew over the fence from nowhere. She brought me some fish and just about had me in her arms, when I heard my mistress say, "Good." In that instant I ran the other direction. Mama Pearl had to leave; my family was worried. They coaxed me for a long time but I ignored them except to watch out that they might catch me. I watched them through the window as they peeked out to see what I was doing. There were so many bugs to catch; I flipped and flopped back and forth over the lawn.

It was 8:00 P.M. Mama Pearl came out again. It was pitch dark by now. She turned on the garden lights and offered me some fish. In a few minutes she had me in her arms. She brought me to my master. My family hugged and kissed me. I looked like an angel so they said. Then they called me a monster and said never again will they leave me out after eating my dinner. My master held me in his arms. I lay on my back and closed my eyes. That day I played more than they ever saw me play. I almost fell asleep. I was so tired that I growled.

My Platform

My family thinks that I am changing. I have my own ideas about certain things. When I wanted to go outside, my mistress picked me up and said, "Cricket, you can't go out." I spoke up and sassed her. When I wouldn't stop, she spanked my behind and said, "Don't you talk to me like that." Later she put my harness on and let me sit on the platform. That was fun. When she came to get me, I said, "No, I want to stay." But I didn't growl. When she pulled me I refused to go. She picked me up and brought me inside.

My master was observing me all the while. He said, "Cricket will always be a naughty kitty." I never act like that to him because he always lets me do what I want to do.

Well, the next morning was very cold. My mistress put on my harness again. I got upset again and growled all the way downstairs. When she put me on the platform, I became more upset. She spanked me again, but I only growled louder. She put her face to me and I sassed her right in her face. She carried me to my room and closed the door. My family was concerned. I never behaved so badly. Was I going to be a problem kitty? Maybe I would not love them anymore. When she returned to pick me up, I ran upstairs happy as a kitten, purring all the way, then lay on my rug.

Finally, the family understood that I tried to tell them it was too cold outside.

Naughty

I have been a naughty kitty. I was outside playing. My mistress called and called me, but I would not come inside. She came again and called. This time she saw me playing with my chum, Tiger. When I started towards home, Tiger cried out, "Don't go" very loudly; of course I stayed.

Papa Otto was in his yard; he heard Tiger and shook his head. The family decided no more running around with wayward kitties; they are naughty and they teach me to be naughty.

After that day I never saw Tiger again. When my mistress inquired about him, she learned that Tiger disappeared. No one ever knew what happened to him. His family is sad. They miss him and will never know what happened to Tiger. I miss him, too. My family is grateful that it was not I who is gone—I am happy with my home. I will never, never leave it.

Little Boy Cricket

My mistress calls me "Little Boy Cricket." I am told by many people that I behave politely and have such intelligence. My master's grandchild came to stay for a few days. We had a good time together. A week after he returned to his home, a friend called my mistress to ask how the little boy enjoyed himself. My mistress said, "Oh, what a monster." Today she made a cake and left it on the table to cool. Whe she returned, she found a big hole in the cake. When she asked him about it, he just looked at her with such a satisfied expression on his face and was not interested in talking about it. It was such a large piece that she scolded him and gave him a laxative. The lady laughed and laughed. The conversation went on. Then my mistress learned her friend was asking about the grandson and not me.

Left Me Again

For two days I watched my family pack their clothes into suitcases. During that time I never left the house for very long. Usually it is a hassle to get me inside, even if they call dinner and I am not hungry. I just don't appear.

The evening before, I followed them all around the house. When they tried to catch me, I did my usual hiding so they would have to find me, but this time I ran under the couch right where they could catch me. My mistress carried me down to my room. Everything was there, ready to put in the car. I didn't jump on my mistress. I just looked at everything, went to the chair near the window, and turned my back on them. My family felt sad.

My family came home! I met them when they came in the garage. I spoke to them and ran upstairs for my dinner. After that they picked me up and loved me. I was so happy, I purred and purred.

For the next four days, I did not go out to play very much. When I did, it was only for a little while, then I would run back to see them.

When my mistress went outside to shop, I was at the garage door crying for her. She heard me crying as she walked across the street, and wondered how I knew she was coming. I could see her through the air vent.

Fleas

Do you know what? I am real proud of my master! My mistress saw me scratching fleas. This time of the year, they are especially annoying. She was busy doing something else, so she picked me up and tossed me in my master's arms and said, "For goodness sake, you must flea Cricket." He tried so hard to find them, but they were nowhere in sight, so I got off his lap, looked him straight in the eyes, and said, "They are right here where I am scratching." Sure enough, he understood clearly. He picked me and found three big fleas. Afterwards, I went right up to thank him. I gave

37

him an extra big kiss on his nose. We both have a good understanding.

Tonight's Episode

This time my master opened the door to close the water spray off the lawn. Just at that moment, I was there and took advantage of it. I slipped through the open door and I was out for another ɛvening spree. The family gave up; they didn't call me because they knew better. By nine o'clock my master beat a jar with a spoon and called, "Dinner!" It was dark now. Suddenly he saw a little animal flying over the fence from Papa Otto's yard. It looked like Pasha and it was. My master invited him upstairs for some food. When they got there, I was in the kitchen waiting for that promise. Evidently I came in first; it was so dark that he didn't see me.

The Aluminum Chair

The family went to visit a sick friend and they took me with them. All went very well; we were sitting in the garden chatting when a kitty came up to us, crying in a small voice. I was sitting on my master's lap and began to growl at the kitty. This disturbed me more and more. I was in a strange place. I got nervous so my master became upset. He said to my mistress, "Please put him in the car. He doesn't like it here." But my mistress ignored that. She just said, "Leave him alone. He has to get used to going out".

The kitty finally went away and my master tied me to an aluminum chair. I began to pull out of my harness. The harness was tightened. This time I took a leap and off I went, dragging the chair with me, crying all the way down the brick steps. My mistress was right behind, chasing me all the way down the stairs, trying to catch the chair. Everyone watched it come tumbling down after me. All was quiet for an instant; then I howled louder than they had ever heard me. By that time my mistress came to the end of the brick steps. I was hiding behind a big bush. The chair was on the last stair. Everyone breathed a sigh of relief. I was not hurt, only frightened.

My Little Friend, Pasha

Pasha has grown up. He is a year old. Ever since he was a kitten, Pasha has always had the best of me. He can't leave me alone, and is always socking me with his claws. Sometimes it hurts and I cry. I guess I just knew he was a baby. Today I learned to defend myself. Even though I am tied up, I win. Before he gets near me, I beat him to the punch. Really, my family is surprised because they saw me give it to Pasha. Now he runs away. Of course we love each other; I miss him when he is away. The family loves him like my little brother. My mistress just looked out the window again. We are sitting at a respectful distance, staring at each other. One hour later and my mistress came out to see me. I was caught and could not move. She removed the knot from my rope and I went directly to my box that Pasha was just going to enjoy and said softly, "This is mine." Of course Pasha moved away. Then he looked at me most intently and moved farther away.

My Master and My Kisses

Now that I am two years old I am learning much more. When I get on my master's lap to love him, he teaches me. He says, "Down, Cricket." Then I lie down. I put my head on his arm and look at him with all my love as he pets me. Today, he put his head down and said, "Kiss me." I raised my head, put my face right up to his nose and gave him a big smack. Later on that evening, my mistress carried me into the den where my master was sitting. It was the usual 8:00 P.M. When I saw him, I jumped out of her arms and snuggled up to my master. I am always anxious to be with him.

Snitching Food

We were having company for dinner—our relatives from London. My mistress made a pumpkin pie. When it was baked she put it in the bedroom and locked the door, so this time I was not going to get into mischief. When she returned I was on the breakfast table. She forgot the sample piece for my master. I got a teenzy-weenzy taste.

T.V.

As I said before, after my misbehavior in the living room with the Persian rugs, I was banished from it because I was so naughty. Ever since I have used all my tricks to get through that wall. Now today a man came with our new T.V. for the living room. The family has never allowed a T.V. there when guests come to visit us; conversation has always come first. Today was the most exciting. I couldn't believe what was going on. Soon I approached the T.V. man, who said hello and patted me. But this is something new! I walked around the T.V., then inspected it from all sides. Finally I went walking up and down, talking in a special voice—one that my family had never heard before. It seemed that I was saying, "Look, look, look—something new is here!" Besides, I was allowed to stay and that was something different. That afternoon, when the family was looking at T.V., I brought out my catnip mouse, then sat in front of the T.V. and played with it. I shook it and tossed it in the air; it was so much fun!

Tricky

My mistress thinks she is very smart because she tricked me again. She went out to get me inside the house, which I usually refuse unless she calls, "Dinner!" Then she got a bright idea. Rather than promise more food when I am just a little overweight, she called out, "Pasha!" In an instant, I jumped over the fence and came running. The trick worked, because she never calls Pasha when we are outside. Anyway, I said, "Here I am," and here I was. Then I saw something different about her. I smelled her new dress and her shoes. She only wears a dress when she is going out. I am glad that I did come home, because we went out for a ride.

Scratching Post

Papa Otto is most interested in my well being. He loves to watch me climb his tree and I always enjoy climbing up to the top, then walking out on the branches. There are always birds there, but I have never caught one. They are too smart for me. Now that I am tied up every day with a ten-foot leash, I don't get to climb any tree. Papa Otto put a long pole eight feet high in my yard. This morning my master saw me sitting on the very tip-top. I looked around, then jumped off. Papa Otto also brought home a piece of wood with lots of bark. Every day I stretch up and sharpen my claws. I have used it so much, there is only the hard wood left, so they will have to find another piece because I enjoy it so much.

Copy Cat

My mistress says that I am getting pretty snippity lately. She picks me up to love me and I cry or growl at her. When she brings me outside—even where I love to be sometimes—I still growl. Just now she gave me a crack on my behind, and said, "No, no." I stared at her with almost a look of guilt because I do love her, so I stopped. You see, I always hear Pasha when he growls at the family for no reason at all. So I guess I am a copy cat. For no reason at all I growl. There is nothing she can do other than to stop me at the time; I really am not angry. It is just the thing for me to do. That is what Pasha does and so I do it.

Pasha and I Ran Away

My mistress put me out in the yard today. Very soon after, she saw me looking from side to side; I seemed disturbed. She came out to see me. It was raining, so in the house I went. Soon we heard Pasha calling me. He has never seen the rain before. He began to cry and was licking his fur. My mistress let him come inside. Later, the family went out for brunch. We stayed downstairs and played. When the family returned, they opened the garage door with the genie. Pasha ran outside in one direction, and I went in the other. My master caught me as I bounded up the street. My mistress chased Pasha and grabbed him as he ran in the other direction. We had so much fun.

A Good Day

Pasha and I had a good day. It was raining and so cold that I had to stay indoors. Pasha, of course, came to play and stayed until evening. Later, the family had to leave; they opened the garage door and Pasha flew out across the street. My mistress was so concerned that she ran after him and picked him up. With that, he took a big bite on her hand and made a bad scratch. My mistress felt badly to think Pasha could be so naughty. The next day she had a new plan. When Pasha came to visit us she let him in the house. He ran in happily. *Now,* she thought, *this is the time to teach him a lesson.* She approached him, and caught him as he growled. She had on some heavy canvas gloves. He growled, screamed, scratched, and bit her hand as hard as he could. My mistress spoke softly to him and petted him as he continued to growl and bite while she held him firmly. Finally he stopped. She put him outside, but he returned right back, looking sweet and happy. He stayed all day without any more problems. My master petted him as lay on the couch. That evening, he refused to go home. He had some more tantrums. On with the gloves again, more screaming and growling, then he calmed down. My mistress thought he has had his lesson, so she tossed him out. Pasha still has some baby ways. His voice goes from low to high key. When he growls, he growls. Sometimes he imitates me. The family gets confused. Now he imitates my cry for food. He is as fat as he can get without popping. His family gives him all he wants to eat, but it seems that everything I do, Pasha wants to do.

Angel

We are expecting someone very special. Our medical friend Uncle Maurice has a little dog named Angel. She is a Yorkshire terrier about one and a half years old. We have never seen her. Soon Uncle Maurice will bring her here. Of course, the family is anxious to meet her; they are curious to see how I will accept Angel.

She came today! I couldn't believe my eyes when she walked in with Uncle Maurice. She came right up to me and said, hello. I was positively shocked. Suddenly my back went up and stayed like that for a long time. My eyes couldn't believe it! Here she was, talking to me. She wanted so much to play and talk with me. This went on for half an hour, then I sat on the television to get a better look at her. She still came to me and I continued to stare with the most unusual expression on my face. My family made such a great fuss over her. I was not at all jealous, just amazed. Then we went to the kitchen. They gave her some dinner while I watched from a distance. She ate all she wanted and when finished, she wanted more. Uncle Maurice was surprised because he had cooked a chicken for her and she would not eat a bit of it. After that I had some dinner too, but not like Angel had. When I was finished, I went up to her dish where she was eating and hissed right in her face. She didn't mind. She kept right on eating; so they gave me just a few bites more. Then Angel barked at me. This was too much for me. I ran out of the kitchen. Everyone was so glad that I should behave so sweetly.

Really, I am not a naughty kitty, and now I am getting used to her. Uncle Maurice and Angel left for the night and will return tomorrow.

Uncle Maurice and Angel came back to see us. As soon as Angel saw me, she said hello to me. My back went up again and I told her off. I cracked her with my two paws. She gave a little cry. Everyone was upset that I should be impolite to Angel, who loves me so much. Just the same I was not sorry. We are having dinner. Now I am sitting on the chair and here is Angel, adoring me again. I can't understand her; how can she like me so much? Uncle John also came to dinner. He is worried about Angel. He thinks I may hurt her, so he got off of his chair and came over to me. He said, "Don't you hurt that little Angel!" He even shook his finger at me. I looked at him as though I knew what he really meant. I haven't hit her again—yet.

All day long, she insists on talking to me. She follows me wherever I go. She really is a sweet, darling, little girl doggie. Right now I am in the den on the television watching her intently; my tail is all fluffed out. I can't seem to get upset with her. I don't growl or hiss as much.

Just now, Pasha walked into the room. He is staring at Angel; he is so shocked that his back is really up. We have never seen anything like this happen to us. Pasha just ran crying downstairs. He was so upset that he left his message on the floor in my room, but he is still crying about Angel. My mistress picked Pasha up and he actually let her hold him without any temper. I guess he wants her to love him too.

Uncle Maurice and Angel came back to visit with us. Of course, Angel wanted to say hello. I am not quite sure about her yet, so up went my back again. In a few minutes I calmed down. We sat near the table for dinner. I was tied to a chair and so was Angel. She sat near Uncle Maurice. I didn't take my eyes off her. There was no hissing and nothing exciting happened. I behaved politely. After dinner my mistress brought our chairs closer while they were playing cards. Really, one can get used to anything, and I think maybe Angel is not so bad after all.

Next morning, Angel wanted her breakfast. My mistress gave me some too. Our dishes were close together. I forgot about everything except the food I was eating. Then what do you think happened? Angel helped herself to my milk. I just backed away and sat there watching her. Isn't that something! Of course, the family was delighted to think that I could behave so sweetly.

Pasha came in and is sitting on the stairs. His back is up again. Angel went over to see him, but Pasha is not interested. I decided to talk it over with Pasha. Angel keeps her distance. Pasha hissed at Angel and gave her two swats. Angel ducked, so he missed her.

Later, the family went out to dinner, and as they were leaving, Pasha slipped in through the front door. As my mistress was locking the door, she heard a distinct "Yip!" Poor Angel—she got it! Back in the house, my mistress came searching for Pasha. She found him downstairs. Of course, after that Pasha was sent home. By now Pasha wanted out, and out he went through my door, and that was the end of that. Angel and I spent the evening together.

The Knapsack

The family called me for a ride, so in the car I hopped. As usual, I enjoyed it very much. We went all the way down Market Street to an art store. When we arrived there, my mistress took me in her arms into the store. Right then and there, I cried out very loudly, "I don't like it in here!" My voice grew louder and louder. The family couldn't just leave for me, so they found a knapsack. They tossed me into it; I was so happy to get in and snuggled up to it. My head was out so I could see everything. Of course, a few customers came up to talk with me. I behaved sweetly. Then we went out to the busy street. I was still in the knapsack. When we got to the car, I easily jumped out into the back seat.

Pasha

As for Pasha, today my mistress again had to spank him and he growled. I watched him, then saw my mistress toss him out the back door. Soon after, my mistress went downstairs to the room. Immediately we heard Pasha crying; then we saw him jump up through the bars of the window and sit on the sill. He looked at us in that intense, naughty way, crying to come in. My mistress ignored him, but I went up to him and said hello through the window glass. Later, when my master took me outside, Pasha heard us, and came running into the house. There he was, back again, lying on my rug, looking so contented.

My Master Spanked Me

My mistress made a harness for me. She put it together with a strip of nylon. She worked hard to fit me. I complained all the while, but there was no concern in her mind that I could pull out, so she worked on. After all my escapes and worries that I gave the family, they were glad that I could not escape again. Today my master put me out in my yard and then left for the afternoon. My master was the "kitty-sitter." He gave me my dinner, which tasted good. After a few hours, my master came to bring me inside. He was surprised when I growled and bit him—not very hard, but enough to show him I was unhappy. My master was shocked. Ever since they brought me home I could always get his sympathy. Now I outright bit him. Of course, he was not going to take that from me. So he spanked me, but not very hard. Then I just looked at him, not ashamed, but I stopped. You see, I love him.

The Family Was Confused

I surely confused the family and my doctor. All the fuss about my bladder and personal habits. This morning my mistress changed the litter green in my comfort box, which had not been changed for a long time because I refused to use it. Well, to the surprised family, they found my little message later in my box. The fact was that perhaps I had no problem at all. I just refused to use that box because it was not in the proper order. Now, every day I repeat my performance. No more problems—the family is positively amazed. I tried so hard to tell them what I thought of my comfort box, and they could not understand me.

Papa Otto and My Master

Papa Otto is so good to me. Today he brought over a thick log covered with green bark. I sniffed at it, but only used my old one—there is no more bark on it and I seem to enjoy it. I have to get used to new things and I am sure I will like my new scratching post.

I am so curious about everything, even though my yard is clean and clear for me to play in. I find a reason to check out anything around, so before I know it, I am tangled up in a shrub or plant in bloom. In this position I can pull out of my harness. Today, Papa Otto and my master moved all the plants farther away, which gives me more room to play. This took a long time to do. But I don't mind, if they have to work so hard. They will do just about anything because they love me.

My Day

The other morning my master said to Pasha and to me, "Now, be good kitties. No fighting." Then he said to my mistress, "Cricket just gave Pasha a crack." They were concerned for Pasha. They thought that I was getting out of hand. Today my family was surprised to see me stand on my hind legs to give Pasha a good swat. Actually, they thought I looked awfully cute. Like the picture of Peter Rabbit, I was standing over Pasha with my paws out; I meant business.

Then this morning, Pasha and I and my family were standing in the hall. My mistress said to my master, "Be quiet; watch and see what happen." Pasha was a few feet away from me. I wanted to get to the kitchen, which, you know, is my favorite place. I was anxious to get there, but I kept my eyes on Pasha, who was sitting like an innocent baby, his little face so sweet. Well, I made a quick run past him. Sure enough, just as I was passing Pasha, he jumped on me with his claws out and dug into me. I cried out. Right then, the family could see the truth. That's why I am defending myself, trying to get in the first swat. Now they feel better about me. After all, I am not such a naughty kitty to start a fight.

My Problem

I was very small when my family had to take me outside on my leash to dig a hole for me. Sometimes I would dig my own. They would coax and coax me; then in that mood I would oblige them. Now, ever since I ate that large slice of pound cake, I have been irregular. It's been three days now, so my family gave me milk, prune juice, and later an herb laxative. The family called the doctor, who said to give me some very rich food. So guess what they gave me. I had some melted butter with half and half. They waited and waited. Well, my mistress got impatient and took me out on my leash. I prepared my place and sat in it. I began to stare and listen. Pasha was on the fence watching me. My mistress coaxed me; I listened more. There was a bird chirping in the tree. I love birds, especially if I could catch one. Myy mistress insisted. I moved to another place.

Of course, I finally did, but don't you think it unusual that I should respond only after all their coaxing?

Next day, my family had to take me back to the doctor; it wasn't the irregularity. The doctor said I had an infected bladder, so now I am taking medication.

My Thoughts

A few days later, we went to see my own doctor. She checked me over carefully. She talked softly and petted me. I was happy—whatever she had to do did not hurt. I think that I had a good time. She told my family to get a lot of vitamin C down me somehow. My mistress followed her instruction. She ground up the vitamins, added water, and poured it in my mouth. I had to swallow it. I was lying on my back; she watched my face pucker up. I didn't say a word, I just glared at her. Next morning my mistress checked my comfort box—it was empty. She said, "Oh, Cricket, you didn't leave anything for me." Now the family was worried. An hour later, I went to my mistress and looked at her so intensely, started downstairs, and turned to see if she was coming. She followed me as I went downstairs to my box. I sat there and looked at her, then walked in. She was so happy as she watched me perform and petted me. The family thought it unusual that I could transfer my thoughts to her.

Peter

I am pretty uptight this morning. I was in my yard enjoying a beautiful day. My mistress was talking with Papa Otto when we all heard a small kitty crying. He came right up to Papa Otto to be loved. My mistress asked him to pick the kitty up for her, and sure enough he did. The kitty is all white, with two black spots around his eyes and a black tail. My mistress took him in her arms and brought him upstairs in the house. I didn't really care, and paid no attention. He must have had a good time because they were together for a long time. Peter has beautiful, fluffy fur. He follows my mistress and master wherever they go. They don't know his name, so my master calls him Peter. He didn't have his real mommy very long, because he likes to nurse on their sweaters and make bread. I am not very kind to Peter—I growl when he comes around. I am still tied outside and Peter is indoors with the family to play. Really, I don't mind in the least, but I don't want either Pasha or Peter around too close. Pasha went upstairs to see what was going on. Soon he ran out screaming and growling. He does not like Peter. He is in the hall growling at him. Then he came out to see me. My mistress saw him stare and stare at me. I think he remembers that last crack I gave him. It isn't that I don't love him. I am a peaceful kitty and like to be good. After that day, we never saw Peter again. Papa Otto thinks he belongs to a family one block away.

49

Noisy Breakfast

As I have said before, I am extremely sensitive. The least bit of noise and I jump. When I am eating, I like everything quiet. But my mistress goes around the kitchen rattling the dishes. Today when I started to eat my dinner, she was fussing around again and this upset me. So I raised my head, turned to look at her, and said "Please be quiet so that I can eat my dinner."

She got the message and replied, "Excuse me, dear. I am sorry," before she realized that I am only a kitty.

More Problems

I was in the kitchen with my mistress as she cleaned the dishes after dinner. There is always a chance that I may get a little something more, and I also look for any leftovers on the dishes, which I usually help myself to when no one is looking. Tonight it was shrimp and my mistress was busy, so I disappeared. Soon after, she heard a muffled cry and a rattling noise. She looked all over for me, calling and calling, like the time she found me in the light well behind the bathroom. She called my master. They were worried. Where could I be? I sounded unhappy. Suddenly my master threw open the dishwasher door and there I was, looking most uncomfortable and upset. I was gingerly standing over those long sharp pickets with my feet barely touching the bottom, my back hunched and head down. My master picked me up as I gave out a frightened cry. After a few minutes, I was feeling all right and went back to some more possible mischief.

Another Lesson

The family was downstairs; I was upstairs in the gym sleeping. Later they heard me crying loudly; they were concerned and came upstairs. But when they saw me, I was peacefully lying in my box. The crying continued, so my mistress opened the front door and who should be there looking like a poor little orphan? No one other than Pasha.

He walked into the room where I was, jumped on the table, and watched me as I lay in my box. Then he wandered into the kitchen and refused some food offered him. The next moment he turned on my mistress, growling—he tried to bite her. He ran into the garage. She picked him up and softly talked to him, then opened the door and put him outside. The family is curious about his moods—they range from a sweet kitty to a very unmanageable little monster.

Donner Lake

The family returned from Reno. Now, a week later, they are busy in the garage with more packing. I know they are going away, so I stay around. For a week, I never take my eyes from the window when I am outside. Every time they look out there, they see me staring and staring in the window. I know they are leaving. It is very cold outside, so I sit in my box. Early this morning at four o'clock, I heard the family moving around; they were busy with packing. I cried once when my mistress came downstairs. She did not answer me, so I stopped crying. I learned never to cry when I am in my room. Ever since I was a tiny kitten, my mistress would never answer me if I cried. So now I know better. Finally, they were ready to drive away and they put me in the car. I was so happy! All the way to Donner Lake I behaved beautifully. I told the family about everything I saw. The big noisy trucks don't upset me anymore. I enjoyed every bit of the ride.

When we arrived at the cabin on the lake, I began to tremble. The family took me out of the car and brought me to our cabin. That was all right, but I was upset because of all the noise. The big lake with water frightened me. I know all about water and the room was strange to me. That evening I did not want to eat dinner; for the first time I refused food. My mistress gave me butter and cream with vitamins. She had to spoon-feed me.

Soon after, Uncle Dan, a very good friend of ours, came to

51

stay with us. I sat next to him while the family played cards. When we had lunch, Uncle Dan gave me a tiny bit. I was hungry by now and asked him for more—of course, I had all I wanted. Everyone was happy to see me well again.

Uncle Dan is a dentist; he was curious about my teeth. When he checked them, he was amazed to see no tartar on them. Of course, I stayed close to him because he is sweet and thoughtful to me.

My mistress keeps me in my harness. She ties me to a chair in front of the window. I am such a fearful kitty that people going by our window or a dog will frighten me, and I pull away. My mistress insists that I must not get so upset. I have been sitting here for a long time now, and today the family noticed that I behave less fearfully. There is so much going on with the birds and the animals that I am beginning to get curious. So my family has decided to expose me to more new experiences. Well, I am not interested in that, but I know just how to worry them and give my mistress something new to worry about in this apartment. All day long I find a way. They usually keep my harness on so I can not get away from this apartment when they are away. They think that I am sure to be here when they return. That is what they think. When they least expect it, I disappear so fast—I can and I do every chance that I get. So I hid in the bathtub. Later they found me in the bathtub. That's my favorite hiding place—behind the shower curtain. So when they look for me again, I am not there; I am in the closet in a box within another box, or in the bathroom on top of a cabinet. This time they searched for a long time. When they looked up above and saw me, I looked at them delighted. My mistress had to climb up on a chair to reach me; the cabinet is eight feet tall. They never know where to look. Each time they go through shock, wondering if I could have run outside.

This morning was the best of all. My mistress looked and called me. She went through all of my hiding places and was truly worried. There were no more places to look for me. Then my mistress saw two little gray paws sticking out behind the refrigerator. She called me and my master called me. I really put one over on them. I was enjoying all this commotion.

My master took a glass of water and poured it in back of the refrigerator. There was no other way to reach me. Instantly they heard a scuffle, then out I came, shaking my wet paws. I was wet. They decided not to laugh out loud, but it was so funny they could hardly keep quiet. They just ignored me in case I might decide to go back in there again. This time I lost.

Naughty Pasha

Pasha was very naughty today. My mistress picked him up to love him. I was tied outside and heard him growl and scream louder than ever. I began to cry and cry. I knew he could hurt her and I was afraid. She had her gloves on and let him have his tantrums. I kept crying. When she came out, she still had him in her hands. Then she tossed Pasha out. I cried so hard, which I usually never do unless I feel like it, that she picked me up. I was so glad to be with her, and I let her hug and kiss me. Pasha is outside now trying to get in the house. No one came to let him inside, so he played in the yard by himself.

My Beauty

Everyone tells me how gorgeous I am, and I really am. I have on my winter coat, which gives me long fur with a special full collar. I look like an aristocrat. I usually behave like one too. My head is held high, with quiet pride and dignity. I speak so softly. Sometimes my voice has a special baby quality. When I get upset and tell my mistress off, my voice becomes strong and decisive.

Shopping Tour

Another day for shopping and again I went with the family. This time my mistress put me in the knapsack and strapped it to her shoulder. I was very good. My head was out and I looked from side to side from my knapsack. The family was busy shopping and sometimes forgot about me. But the shoppers didn't. They stopped to talk to me. I took them by surprise when they patted me; I loved it! Then we went back to the car. They took me out of my knapsack so I could walk. For the first time I walked without pulling back, but I was not always sure which car was ours. Really, we all enjoyed an exciting adventure.

My Food

The family enjoys eating out. They often bring me home choice bits. Once the portion lasted four days; then they offered me the usual kitty food. I looked at it and turned my head. That day I didn't eat very much until my mistress picked me up and said, "You eat!!" I had to. She kept opening my mouth and stuffing it in. I had to swallow it. My family decided they were not going to spoil my good habits. Now when they bring home filet, it is offered only in small portions, then frozen for a later, special treat.

The Runaway

I gave the family a bad time today. I was outside all day. When I came inside I had a few bits of food from the table, which does not happen very often. The family was going out that evening, so they made preparations. Just before they were leaving, my master opened the door to water the garden. Right then I was ready to go through the door and I did. My master called me back, but I turned to look at him, swished my behind, and then took off. It was 6:30 P.M. They had a special date to keep. My mistress decided to stay and coax me back. She called and Mama Pearl called me, but I gave no signs of obeying. By eight o'clock they heard me jumping over the fence into our yard. I stood there and teased them. I don't get away very often and this was quite a treat. They say I am very stubborn; and I was, just keeping my distance. Even dinner could not interest me. When all hope was lost, I darted past them and made it back home. Mama Pearl said, "Quick, lock his door," and my mistress did.

Pasha and Poncho

This morning I was in my yard, lying in my box on a warm carpet. It was wet after a heavy rain; I felt so good in the sunshine. Then Pasha came over to see me. Before he could get too close to me, I jumped up and chased him away. Today he was not going to push me out. I returned to my box. Soon a new kitty sat on the fence, looking curiously at me. He is white with black spots on his back; he has such long fur. My mistress picked him up and petted him for a while. My master named him Poncho. As my mistress walked away, she heard a loud cry. It was Poncho. Pasha took a swipe at him. Poncho just sat there, looking so startled.

My Real Mother

I was so small when my family picked me up that I forgot I had a real mother. She must have been very clean, because I am so fussy about my toilet. She taught me my bathroom manners. I have never made a mistake in the house. We were in my playyard yesterday. My master had to move a large plant to make room for me to play. He moved it farther away. Soon afterward, I prepared for my daily business. When my master turned to look for me, I was in the hole doing my duty; all he could see was my head and shoulder.

Margaret

My mistress came to my room early one morning to call me for breakfast. She was surprised to see all the canned food on the floor in the hall. The packaged food was scattered all over.

Some of the packages were open and others partly eaten. Of course, I was to blame as the thief, but when my mistress opened the door, I was in my room waiting for her. No one could solve the mystery. That evening, my family went out for dinner. When they returned about 10:00 P.M., I flew out of the garage—something I never do, because I am very afraid of the street and the noise. Again, the next morning more food was opened and scattered on the floor. The family checked the backyard. There were large footprints all over. Then they realized that we have a visitor from the park, a raccoon. They called the SPCA, who brought a cage to trap our visitor. Next morning at four o'clock, my master heard a loud scream. Sure enough, we caught the thief and it was a raccoon. My master called her Margaret. She had lined the cage with torn newspaper and a dirty rag used for shoe polish as a nest. Then she ate the food and was trapped. She looked like she was expecting babies. Her screams were loud and angry. Later the neighbors were invited to meet Margaret. They were curious. She gave a great performance. She hissed and growled. Soon the truck came to take Margaret away. She seemed very calm when the lady picked up the cage. There was no screaming. She just lay comfortably and was carried away. The lady explained that she could smell other animals on her. So Margaret was not afraid.

The Shower Stall

Today I was a naughty kitty. I growled at my mistress because she would not let me outside. When she scolded me I wouldn't stop, so she put me in the shower stall with a rug to sit on. Usually when my mistress does this, I cry, "Please let me out." After a while she will open the door and say to me that I must be a good boy. This time I was in the stall for only a few minutes. Then I pushed the door open and ran out. My mistress caught me as I made my way down the hall, then tossed me back in. She had a rope and began to tie up the door. *Now,* she thought, *this will hold him.* But this was not so. While she was working on the door, I leaped over it and ran off, then hid where she could not find me for a little while. Of course, I won that time. My mistress did not have the heart to spoil my victory, and maybe I deserved it. I outsmarted her.

Pasha

Pasha saw my mistress hold and love me. He was on the floor and looked up to her, staring so wistfully, wishing he could be loved like me.

Lakeport

My master loves me so much. Ever since I was small he has always protected me; whenever my mistress tried to expose me to a new experience, like other places and animals, he would always would say "No. Cricket might get hurt or frightened." So now I am a real fraidy kitty. I am afraid of noise, new places, and animals. Now my mistress insists that I should be exposed to everything so I will learn there is nothing to be afraid of. Today she put me out on the lawn near our room in a motel. I was so frightened that I cried and cried. Now I am afraid of the lake and all the ducks. There is also the terrible noise from the motorboats. I cringe when they pass by.

There are about fifteen ducks here. All are boys except two girls. My mistress is feeding them graham crackers. So far, all the boys came with the two girls. They are dying to pick up some large crumbs, but they are afraid. I am scared, and sit here in my box under a table, hiding and crying. So far only one girl came to eat. My mistress tossed out more food. They came closer and closer. The boys are afraid of me; all they do is talk about me and stare. They are wishing they could have a bite to eat. Just now a girl ate from her hand while I looked on. I am getting a little used to them, but the boys are still fearful of me.

The next day, the other girl came to my mistress and ate from her hand. One boy came up and took a piece of cracker a few feet away from her.

The girl ate ten crackers. My mistress wondered where she put them.

They Chased Me

Today is Saturday.

The family returned from the dinner party. I was alseep when they came in. Some friends came in to visit the family; of course, I got more attention. Soon after, while no one was looking, I slipped out the door to see outside. Someone said, "Cricket got out."

My family and Uncle Dan set out to catch me. It was pitch dark. My mistress had a flashlight. Again I was free to run, and I did. I ran to the right, and to the left into the bushes, and around some cottages. In one house, there was a huge basement wide open for me to investigate. They could never have found me. I turned away and ran across the street. Uncle Dan was on the road trying to stop me, but I made it across the dirt road to a large home. Soon, large dogs began to bark. The owners turned on the lights to see what the commotion was about. Their yard was huge. My family followed me. When they least expected it, I stopped to rest, then they caught up with me. I allowed them to almost catch me. Then I popped up, to run in another direction. Back to the dirt road. Uncle Dan held his flashlight, prepared to warn oncoming automobiles. Suddenly, right then and there, I dropped down on the side of the road and invited my master to pick me up. Of course, everyone was happy. I was a naughty kitty. They held me tightly. How could they trust me?

After our party last night, my mistress put on my harness and tied me to a picnic table with my box so I could nap. I am not frightened anymore, but I want to be in our room with the family, so I have been crying a little.

Soon after, my mistress heard a man talk to me; he promised to come and get me. She did not pay much attention to that. She was busy and forgot about me. My master was still asleep. Ten minutes later, she peeked out to see if I was all right and enjoying the sunshine. To her horror, I was gone. My mistress knew who took me. She ran upstairs to question the man, but he denied it. She also checked with the guest in the next room and received the same answer. By this time, my mistress was hysterical. She spoke to the manager, who does not like cats; he had no sympathy. She returned to our room and awakened my master; they were both shocked. Then my mistress remarked loudly that we could report it to the police. My master said—also in a loud voice—"Yes, we will call the police." They took the automobile license number.

The man who had stolen me heard my family talking. He was frightened and let me out a few minutes later. My master said, "There he is." I was walking down the stairs, going to our room. My head and my tail were down. I was frightened and shocked. My mistress ran to me and picked me up in her arms; she held me closely. My master hugged me as we returned to our room. It was very early in the morning. I was still in a daze, but so happy to be home with my family.

The Coat Hanger

This was a big day for me and it was hectic. We went out for a ride to do some errands. Soon we stopped at the grocery store. As the car came to a stop, a wire coat hanger that was on top of the back seat fell on me. I jumped! My mistress heard the noise and looked back. I was so frightened, I ran around inside the car hysterically, jumping up and down. Then I sat crouched in a corner, staring at it. I couldn't move. My eyes were wide open. I was terrified. I was trembling and couldn't stop. By this time, my surprised family was concerned. They had never seen me behave like this, even as a kitten. I have always been high strung and frightened at the least noise. This was so dramatic and upsetting that my mistress picked me up to calm me and brought me toward the front seat where she sat. There was a paper bag on the floor at her feet. I was so hysterical that I grabbed her and held on with my claws, still staring at the paper bag. She got a scratch over her eyelid and some on her face. I was still shaking. My master walked to the back of the car and quietly picked up the coat hanger, hiding it behind his back, so I could not see it, then he put it in the trunk of the car. By that time, I was crouched near my mistress in the front seat. My family petted and talked to me, I felt better, but was still frightened.

When we arrived home, I got out of the car. Suddenly I jumped up and down, again and again, walking backward, dragging my leash, staring at it as though it were a snake. My fright was still with me. They unhooked the leash. Then my mistress carried me outside in the fresh air and sunshine.

My Bathroom Manners

My mistress put me in my yard this morning. As usual, I started to dig my place. The earth was too hard to dig very deeply, but I sat down anyway. She left me and went back to the house. Then she turned to look at me as she reached the door to see if all was well. It wasn't. She didn't say "Good boy." So I got up and moved away. She returned with the shovel and dug all around me. Of course, this is just what I wanted, so I sat right down to business.

I Am Learning

I am tied outside again, enjoying the fresh air. My mistress has two cardboard boxes for me to stay in. They are scattered around. I use them all, depending on my moods. My mistress puts me into one of the boxes where I usually stay for a long time. Sometimes I stare into the windows looking for the family. I was sitting in one just now when Pasha got on my roof and poked his paws inside. Of course, he got me out of it, so we had a hassle. Then I went into another box and got into it. Later my mistress went into the house. Pasha followed her. I heard my mistress say she would give him something to eat, and she did. Soon after, he came running out to me. He put his mouth right under my nose so I could smell his breath. I took a good sniff; he had some soup meat. I didn't mind because I had already had my dinner, which was some roast beef and canned chicken with yellow squash.

Sponge Bath

It has been so hot. When I go outside, the ground is dusty. My mistress takes me in and usually gives me a sponge bath by rubbing my fur with a wet rag. After my bath, the rag is very dirty. That's what I get on my mistress when she picks me up. It means a clean blouse every day for her. Today was worse—it is the fleas; she and my master caught twenty-five all together. So she gave me one real bath. I complained, but she held me firmly. Afterwards, I was happy to be clean.

My Spanking

Pasha and I were in the den, lying on the couch. I misbehaved; I was growling at him. My mistress spanked me. Pasha watched her. He looked happy. This was great! I really believe he enjoyed her doing this to me.

Escape

It is 7:00 A.M. The day is rainy, so my mistress tied me close to the window under the eaves outside. When she returned fifteen minutes later, I was hanging by my harness. My feet were barely touching the cement. I was trying to see if my mistress was around, and she was. So I hung there, looking like a little jackrabbit ready for skinning. I didn't want to stay outside, but my mistress insisted that I must, because when I am indoors I usually sleep a lot. So she tied me up again.

Evidently I didn't like it, so off I went. When my mistress returned for me, she found my empty harness hanging on our neighbor's fence. She called several times, and she even said, "Dinner," but I didn't answer. I didn't come. Later Papa Otto said, "Let's ask Mama Pearl to call him." Mama Pearl called for me; soon I came running down Papa Otto's tree. They took me inside and telephoned my family to come and pick me up. On their way downstairs, my mistress heard Mama Pearl say, "I don't think Cricket wants to come home." My family was there to greet me. Sure enough, I didn't want to go home. Mama Pearl and Papa Otto came together. Mama Pearl had me in her arms. As soon as I saw my mistress, I began to growl. My mistress took me in her arms. Both Mama Pearl and Papa Otto were looking so intensely at me. They smiled at me like proud parents. They rescued me and they loved it. When we got upstairs in the house, I continued to growl. My mistress put me in the shower stall. This time I knew what to do. I just jumped over the shower and went straight to my bed. I forgave my mistress when she looked at me and smiled.

Cheesecake

I had another big surprise! Our dear little friend, Mary, who comes to see us often brought a large box and handed it to my family. When she opened the box, to my unbelievable eyes, out popped Cheesecake. Who do you think she is? You can never guess! She is a French rabbit, a beautiful light brown and white. Her fur is so soft. Of course, you know why Mary brought her here—just to see what I would do. Well, believe it or not, I didn't do anything; I just stared at her. She paid no attention to me because all she could think of was the carrot she was eating. Actually, that's all she did for one hour. You would think that she was going to pop, but she didn't. Mary put her and the carrot right up to my nose and Cheesecake was crunching that carrot right in my ears. I never heard such a sound. I didn't say anything to her, but I did growl at my mistress to please leave me alone. The family was surprised to see that I should be considerate and polite. Cheesecake is really a funny rabbit. She went hopping down the hall, sniffing the rug. I was curious to see what she was sniffing, so I followed her, sniffing the rug too.

An Evening Out

This afternoon, I got away again. My leash, which is made of nylon cord, was twisted every which way to prevent any more escapes. Still, it was not tied carefully enough. So off I went on another spree in the early evening. The family didn't bother to call me. They know better by now. My mistress was in my room at her desk when she looked out of the window. She saw a beautiful kitty tripping at a fast pace down the sidewalk in our yard. He looked so intelligent and elegant. He knew where he was going. Pasha was right behind, following him. When they got to the window, my mistress recognized me. I looked tan and cream in the dark dusk. She watched us trot past our window, completely ignoring her. Then we jumped on Papa Otto's platform and sat there, looking at her like two impudent urchins asking her, "What do you want?" My mistress was careful not to sound enticing or anxious; she suggested some dinner. I thought it over carefully as she called me again from inside the house. I was convinced and came running in, with Pasha at my side.

Impatient

I get so impatient with my mistress. Every morning it is the same hassle when she tries to put my harness on. It requires a lot of thought—which way to get it on so I won't slip out. We go through this routine every day. I am really pretty slick about escapes. Just when she thinks I am safely tied for the day, she looks out to see how I am doing, and I have escaped again. Today I was tied up on the lawn in the next-door neighbor's yard. My family left for an hour; when they returned, I was gone. Two men were cutting the lawn. They said that when they came in the yard I was very frightened. Maybe I remembered being tied in Lakeport when the man stole me. Well, this time no one was going to steal me. I pulled and pulled and wiggled my way out. I didn't go very far. When the family called me, I popped up from Papa Otto's yard. Pasha, my good little friend, was with me.

I Was Wrong

This morning after my breakfast, my mistress met me at the door in the hall. She invited me in, but I stood there and looked at her. I knew she would trap me. This time I was wrong, because I got my usual milk with vitamins. They always keep their word, even if it is a trick.

I Sassed My Mistress

My mistress had me by my harness. We were going downstairs on our way to the car. Pasha greeted me with a soft voice. We stopped and kissed, then I pulled away. Pasha wanted more affection, but I pulled away again. I said, "I am sorry, we are going out," and went to the car.

Later, when we returned, Pasha met us at the door. We kissed again and went out to the yard. He was in a good mood. We went out once more for a little while, then my mistress put me out again in my cozy box with a rug to lie in if the wind blew over me. But I didn't appreciate that. I sassed her with a big hiss. My mistress was shocked and scolded me.

My Master's Socks

So often my mistress finds a missing sock belonging to my master on the floor with a big hole in it. I do enjoy his socks and chew holes in them. I went downstairs to the laundry room. My mistress followed me to see what I was doing. I saw the laundry hanging on the line. My master's trousers were there. I passed under them and gave them a crack with my paw. Then I saw his sock and took a swing at it. Later, of course, the sock came down and I chewed another hole in it. Am I a naughty kitty?

Copper Chain

The family bought a twelve-foot copper chain so I could have a longer leash. It is light and does not get dirty. Today I broke the chain. I didn't know it was broken, so I wandered around dragging the chain. My master took advantage of this and quickly grabbed the left-over chain. Now I am back in the house until the chain is repaired.

Later, Papa Otto was ready to give me my dinner. My master untied me from the post to eat. Well, you know how excited I get. I pulled my master as fast as he could run to get my dinner; on the way, the chain broke again. Of course, it is useless. Really, I must be a strong kitty. There is no way to mend it, so they have to find another way. Oh, dear, I give my family lots of problems; they think so, too.

Pasha

Pasha came to see us again today. We had lots of fun chasing each other up and down the hall. Today I got a little bit rough. I chased Pasha and dug my claws into his fur. Of course, he screamed just like I used to when he hurt me. The second time I did it, my master came up to me and said, "No, no. Poor Pasha." Pasha went to the front door to go home. I looked at him unconcerned. I guess I am just a naughty kitty. Anyway, my mistress picked Pasha up and gave him something good to eat. Then she opened the door so he could go home.

Breakfast

What am I going to do with my mistress? She still tries to pull all those tricks on me. But I am on to her. I always have oatmeal mush with milk and moist food. Every morning I can't wait to eat it and every morning my mistress says to herself, *What will he do today?* You see, she is still pouring all those vitamins into my food. So she is quite concerned, and wonders how long I will eat it.

Well, today I ran in for breakfast, looked at my dish, then went to her and said no. Do you know what she forgot? It was my moist food. Then she remembered and gave it to me. Of course, I ate up my breakfast. I really appreciate it very much when she understands.

Another Sponge Bath

Every day when I go out to play I enjoy rolling in the dirt, especially when my mistress is watching. When I return to the house, my mistress picks me up in her arms and in an instant her clothes are very dirty. She decided to wash me before allowing me the house freedom. She picked me up and held me over the washbasin. I stared at the basin because I know it is very wet. When she put me down in the basin I screamed, "No! No!" But she only washed my fur with a damp rag.

Family Went Away

The family went away for three days. When they returned, I didn't make so much fuss over them. The family thinks that I am angry with them because they did not take me. Now my family is going away again. I know it because they are packing. Everything is scattered around, ready to be put into the car. That makes me upset. Everyone can see this because most of the day when I am outside I sit in my box, or the lawn, and stare into our windows. Papa Otto says this is something new. I am really quite nervous at this time. The family wanted to take a picture of me with Mama Pearl. She held me close like she always does. My master held up some food which I never refuse. This time I just looked at it and turned my head. They got the picture all right, but not the one they wanted. I guess I must be a very loving kitty.

Personal Habits

Mama and Papa Otto love me very much, so they often look out the window in the morning to see what is going on. I don't always talk about my personal habits, but when they told my family about Pasha, everyone laughed. I was going to do my usual thing this morning. I dug a nice place for myself. Then Pasha came right over before I could use it, and sat down in my hole that I dug for myself. Of course, I had to make another one.

The Fight

My mistress took me out this morning to my yard. When she opened the door, Pasha was there to greet us. I growled at him, then we kissed. Right after that, I gave him a crack with my paw and Pasha returned it. Then I was tied up for the morning. All was peaceful, then my mistress went upstairs. Soon after, she heard a dreadful scream. She flew downstairs, thinking a stray cat was attacking me. When she got to the yard, I was sitting there watching Pasha really giving it to a strange kitty. The kitty ran to another yard. Pasha followed him off, screaming in such language. The kitty screamed too, and ran to another yard. Pasha came back happy. I wonder, was he protecting me? I was tied up.

Bambi

I was surprised today when Uncle Maurice came to see us. He did not have Angel with him. Angel just does not have good house manners. Wherever she pleases, she leaves a puddle and sometimes worse. Of course, Uncle Maurice gets embarrassed when he goes visiting. One never knows when. Today I was more surprised to see a little thing come tripping behind him on a leash. It looked strange with so little fur. She is a tiny puppy, six months old. Of course, you can guess what I did. Today my fur is still up because I am scared to death of her. At first, she came toward me. I sniffed at her as she came closer—we almost kissed. Everyone thought we were going to be friends. We could have, but when she let out that yip and bounced around me, I got terrified. It isn't her, but that strange noise she makes, so I hissed at her. Later I was in the hall, and she came bouncing after me, so we both ran faster. I was trying to get away from her. Finally, the family found me on the dining-room table looking very upset. Uncle Maurice went to a meeting and left Bambi with my mistress. She cried and cried. Finally, my mistress put her in the closet. That stopped her. So she is back in the living room. She still wants to be with me but I flatly refuse. Worst of all, she left a puddle in the patio on my rug. Just wait until her father hears about this! The family came home from a shopping tour. Bambi was in the bathroom and I stayed in my room. Bambi was so happy to see me that she chased me all the way down the hall. I was so frightened that I spat and hissed at her. My mistress was fearful that I might hurt her. She was really upset and she chased both of us. Finally, I got to the door, which was opened for me, and here I am in my room.

What do you know! Bambi is back again. Just when I was enjoying the patio and the sunshine, in she walked—or, rather, my mistress put her here. You remember I told you about our lovely couch and what Angel did to it? My mistress said no more running around our house.

She is the same Bambi, the usual crying. Really, it is nerve-racking to hear her "yip, yip" constantly. Not only that, she did her little thing on my rug, which keeps me warm when it is cold. All Uncle Maurice can think about her is how cute she is. Well, the yipping went on just so long, then both of us were tossed downstairs. Her screams were so loud that my master came down to rescue me, but I was nowhere in sight. They called, "Dinner!" Still, no sight of me. Now the family was confused. I always came for dinner. An hour later, my master found me on the washing machine and brought me upstairs. Do you know what! They really believed that I was not only bored with Bambi, but I was a little bit jealous.

My Nap

Often my mistress has tried to take me to bed with her for a nap. For some reason or other, when I am not in the mood, I just don't want to, and I pull away. My mistress is firm. She holds me down. She watches me from the corner of her eye. Then I pretend that I am asleep. My eyes are closed, but my tail is wagging. When I think she is asleep, I jump off and run away. Well, she finally gave up. Now I am tied in the yard; she does not invite me anymore. The other day I was outside and I saw Pasha go into the house. He was inside for a long time. Can you imagine Pasha sleeping with my mistress? After all his screaming and tantrums? My mistress prepared to lie down for a nap. She was falling asleep when she felt a soft bundle at her side. Yes, it was Pasha, and he was there a long time. Really, the family was surprised. Now for the past month or so I usually sit in my box, looking into our window. Whenever the family looks out, there I am, staring. Today it was cold and windy, so my mistress brought me inside and lay me on the couch; then she left the room for a few moments. When she returned to the room, I was making bread on the blanket. Then we both went to sleep. Now the family wonders, Do kitties talk to each other?
Ever since then, I am always there, waiting for my mistress to take a nap. When she comes into the room, I have the most unusual expression on my face: "This is my place."

The Lamp

My mistress put a new standing light over the chair where I lay. The globe is very bright since there is no shade, just a small hood. I stared and stared at the light. The next morning, the light was not on. My mistress looked up from her reading to see a most peculiar expression in my face. I could not understand where the light went. She turned the light on for me to see and I seemed satisfied. After that time I never looked for the light when the lamp was not lighted.

Pasha's Cold

Pasha was at our front door again. The family didn't want me to catch his cold, so they would not let him in the house. He cried and cried. My mistress watched me as I went to the door and tried to open it with my paws, but it was closed tight. Pasha had to go home.

Whistling

My mistress took me outside this morning for you-know-what. I made a big place for myself and sat down. I followed a bird with my eyes as it passed by, while my mistress observed a spider rushing out of the hole from behind me before it would drown. Then my mistress began to whistle to a little bird in the tree. This upset me. I didn't know what to do, and had to sit there until I was finished. Just as soon as I could, I dashed home as quickly as possible, pulling at my leash. I never heard such a sound before coming from her.

More Snitching

My mistress came into the kitchen after a long silence from me. There was some meat in the pot on the stove. The heat was turned off. The meat was still warm. When she saw me, I was in the breakfast room holding a big piece in my paws. She took it away from me, then looked on the floor to my accomplice. Pasha was sipping up the gravy that I had dropped on the floor. My mistress didn't bother to scold me. What's the use? I am always doing the wrong thing at the right time—when she is not looking.

I Won

I was outside in my yard today, sitting on my sack. Pasha came over to stop by. This time I was all ready for him. I made a lunge at him. He ran away; I was tied and near the end of my rope, but I got him first and gave him a good swat. Pasha just lay on the ground and said nothing, just like I used to do. Then we both sat down and stared at each other. Pasha really loves me. He is always staring at me; I love him too.

My Birthday

Today is my birthday. This is the happiest day I have ever had. I am three years old. The family gave me a birthday party. All day I knew something was going on. The dining-room table was set for a party, so I sat in my usual chair and stayed there until they came. Mama Pearl and Papa Otto came to my party. After everyone finished eating, my mistress brought in my birthday dinner, which was corned beef and cabbage. When she came in with my dish, it had three candles burning. They all sang, "Happy birthday, Cricket. " Of course I seemed happy to see my dinner come, but when I saw three lighted candles, I was really curious. When my mistress blew out the candles, I began to eat while everyone watched me. It was so good that I gobbled it down. Later we sat around the card table. I got so excited when my master brought in my gifts. I didn't know which to choose. They were four stuffed catnip animals, all standing in a row. I stood there looking so happy and finally chose the yellow bear with brown ears, a button nose, and a yellow coat. I carried it to my pillow on the chair next to Mama Pearl and played with it. Later, when everyone turned to see what I was doing, I was sound asleep, hugging my bear with my two front paws. I was tired out with all the excitement. After the card game was over everyone turned to look at me; they were positively shocked to see my bear with a big hole in his tummy. I must have eaten some of whatever it was inside the yellow coat.

I Am Free

Today I was really surprised! I have been giving the family so many problems with my running away when I am tied in the yard that finally they gave up. You see, there is no way to keep me tied. I can get out of any harness or rope that is tied on me whenever I please. By now they know that they can't win, so today my mistress just opened the door and let me go through.

I couldn't believe that I was free, and just stood there for a minute, then took off. The family is waiting to see how much I will weigh when I return home. That is the problem. I am allowed so much food, which is nourishing, and must remain a certain weight. But, with such nice neighbors around, I could get a handout. Later, my master called me to dinner; in an instant I was there. Of course, they were surprised with such obedience; or let us say that maybe I was just hungry.

I Did It Again

I really worried the family today. You know how careful they are about my personal habits ever since I fell out of the car when I was little.

Today they brought me outside and coaxed me, but I was not in the mood. There was a kitty on the fence watching me. Then I saw a butterfly and chased it. I don't often get outside to play; then there are the flowers to smell. I especially like the hydranges. They are my favorites. When I was finished with all this and no results, the family was worried, so they called my doctor. He was concerned and told them to bring me to his office immediately for emergency.

We got in the car and off we went in a hurry. There is always an emergency box for me in the car. When I saw it, I decided to perform, and I did. I love to do this when the car is moving. My feet were wet but I didn't mind. When the family told the doctor about me, he smiled. His nurse said, "He just wants to give you a bad time," and I sure did. Now, don't you think I am a monster?

A Snack

Pasha and I came in from playing outdoors. We were both hungry, especially Pasha, who kept insisting, so my mistress gave us some dry food. When I saw how much she gave Pasha, I knew he had more than I did. I kept watching him as we ate. My head moved back and forth from my dish to Pasha's. Soon mine was all gone and Pasha was still eating his, slowly and daintily. My mistress did not give me anymore. She just hugged me and said, "You have had enough." I am always hungry, even after eating a big meal, and this was only a snack. You see, my mistress has to watch my weight because I am inclined to get fat. Today, we both had a special treat again. It tasted good as I gobbled mine. Pasha sniffed at his, then he began to nibble. By that time I was finished, so I went over to help Pasha eat his. Pasha was generous but my mistress picked me up and said, "No, no," then hugged me.

Personal Habits

I guess I must be a spoiled kitty. This morning it was raining, but my mistress brought me outside to leave my morning message. She waited to take me back inside. When I was finsihed, I looked at her straight in the face and said, "Meow," which meant, "You can cover it." When she insisted that I must have good manners, I refused. So my mistress had to do just as I ordered.

Our Visit with Dan and Myia

Today we visited Uncle Dan. He lives in a big condominium high up in the sky. When we arrived, the door man came out to greet us, then drove off with our car. By that time I was upset and let everyone know. I howled as we went into the entrance hall. The doorman was surprised to see a kitty with a harness and leash. Usually I am much more friendly, but this time I had my troubles; so I ignored my admirers and kept on crying. We got to the elevator and I didn't like that very much. When Uncle Dan came to the door, my mistress carried me to the living room. It was a very warm day. I ran to the glass door; I was on the way to the porch. My mistress rushed to close it before I got there. Everyone was relieved. The porch was not closed in and we were on the twentieth floor. Then my mistress brought me in to meet Myia, a Siamese kitty, who belongs to the housekeeper. We came into the kitchen. Myia peered out from her home in a cupboard. She is a one-person kitty. For three years, Uncle Dan cannot get near her. She will fly out at anyone and attack. I was still crying but she did not bother to look at me. She stared at my mistress, who put me down, so I ran into the living room crying more. Myia was sitting straight up, with her head turned slightly to the side. She stared and stared without saying a word. My mistress felt her hypnotic stare, as though she was in a trance. A witch with an expression of the past, present, and future in her eyes—yet a human expression. Never did my mistress see such a hypnotic veil of intelligence. She felt drawn into a mystic experience with a cat. Those eyes penetrating with the look of a seer, as long as my mistress observed her, Myia would not change her expression, flinch, or blink her eyes. She had complete command.

Later, when my mistress returned to the kitchen, she tried to talk with Myia, but she had changed her mood. She was lying down. Her head was down, her eyes closed. Nothing could bring back that mood. She was bored and let us know it.

After that exciting performance, I came back to my mistress, still upset. She picked me up and put me in the sink. Then she poured the cold water from the faucet on my head.

I was very wet and stopped crying. Maybe it was the surprise, but I quieted down. My mistress put me in the bathtub behind the shower curtain. I lay there quietly. Then she gave me dinner—I ate most of it.

The family said I passed the test one hundred percent. I am learning the ropes. Then everyone sat down to play cards.

My Illness

I have told you many times how hungry I am in the morning. This morning my mistress opened my door to give me breakfast. When I saw my dish, I passed by it without even a taste. My mistress was surprised. She offered it to me again, but I refused it again. She rushed to my master to tell him; they were worried about me. My eyes were barely open and I was breathing heavily. My mistress put me in a box with her robe to lie on. I looked so weak. It was 6:00 A.M. They rushed me to emergency hospital. The doctor said, "He has pneumonia," and said to spoon-feed me. Later they brought me to my doctor. He also said it was pneumonia. The next morning, I was weaker; they found me lying in the hall. I was trying to walk to them and I collapsed. Of course, they were frightened. This time another doctor checked me. She took blood tests and X-rays; my temperature was 106°. The family was frantic. They had to wait for the test results, which finally came—one was positive. I had infectious peritonitis. When the family came to see me in the hospital, I was still in my box with the robe to lie on. I just stared at them and said nothing. They were shocked and rushed out to buy me some shrimp, which my mistress liquified in cream and spoon-fed me.

There were four other little patients in their cages. They all stared at my mistress. She felt their illness and loneliness. Their silent cry was painful to the family. This was too much for them. They decided to take me home; they would not stay another minute. For four days, I was in critical condition. My mistress got up several times at night to give me antibiotics. She kept pouring liquified liver with cream and vitamins in my mouth night and day.

On the fourth day, I looked better. After the fifth day, I was able to eat by myself. The family was so grateful to have their little Cricket feeling better. Now I am feeling fine.

My Convalescence

I am well recovered from my illness, but my family still worries about me. The other day it was foggy and cold. I spent a lot of time just sleeping. My mistress became worried, so she tried to take my temperature. Of course, you must know what a difficult task it is. I screamed with pain; my eyes were wide with suffering. My mistress tried to comfort me, but I took her hand in my mouth to bite her. She looked at me with such concern. Instantly I flashed a look of understanding. I remembered that I love her and only took her hand lightly with my teeth. My family was amazed and touched with my intelligence. Best of all, I didn't have a temperature.

Misbehaving

My family has the same old problem with me. Sometimes when my mistress holds me, I get excited. Maybe it's because I left my real mother when I was very young, so I make up for it with my mistress. I still insist on kicking and biting her. Today she got a bright idea when I began my usual routine. She said softly, "Good boy, Cricket," instead of scolding me. I stopped instantly—that seemed to have an effect on me. I don't want to be a naughty kitty.

My New Playyard

Regardless of how much I have eaten, I watch the kitchen with that sweet, mournful look that makes my family feel guilty, as though I have not eaten for a week.

My new playyard is the patio. One window faces the kitchen, the other faces the breakfast room. You can bet your life I am right there to see what goes on. When my mistress is in the kitchen, I have my nose glued to the window, looking for a handout. This disturbs her. There is no way to stop me. Sometimes it gets too warm, so she opens the window just a little. I stare and stare at my mistress, which makes her feel uncomfortable. I have had all the food that is coming to me. Yet here I am, with my face peeking through the crack and all she can see is one eye and my nose. Now she closed the window, but I can still see her. Now she draws the shade down. Of course, I never give up, so I follow the shade with my eyes. Finally there is just a crack open, so she can see what she is doing in the kitchen. Well, that is still not enough—here I am with my eyes peering under the shade. By this time, my mistress has had it. Down goes the shade—there is no more for me to see through that window—but there is the breakfast room. I can watch them there; every bite they take. I know the milk carton. I know just about everything that they are eating.

Down goes that shade. Now the family can turn on the lights and forget about me so they can eat. But—that isn't the end. They can still hear my persistent cry. Of course, they won't abandon me. When they are finished, I always get a teensy, weensy bit.

Thanksgiving

The family went out for Thanksgiving Day. They left me all alone. Mama Pearl and Papa Otto gave me my dinner. When my family returned, they stopped at the garage door and opened it with the genie. There I was, waiting for them. Before they could get out of the car, I decided to seek adventure. It was seven o'clock and very dark; up the street I ran with both of them chasing me. I ran in and out of the driveways. When they went one way, I darted another way. I hid in all the bushes, then pounced out just as they got near me. The family thought they would never get me. When I got almost to the end of the houses, I ran back and forth as fast as I could. Finally, I decided to run home and I did.

Maybe I was annoyed that they should leave me so long. They picked me up and hugged me. Then my mistress put me in my room.

I Asked

My mistress was in the kitchen preparing breakfast. As usual, I was hanging around. She got busy and did not pay attention to my cries. How could she know that I was asking for milk? The half-and-half carton was on the table and I was sitting next to it. Soon she heard a familiar noise and came running to see. There was the milk, pouring out all over the table and onto the floor. I was drinking as fast as I could. My mistress couldn't scold me; I asked her for it, so I helped myself when she didn't give it to me. Pasha is much more polite than I am. He comes in and asks for food, but he never steals it.

Pals

Pasha and I have been inseparable for so long. Now, ever since I was ill, the family keeps a watchful eye on me. It is always the patio for me. Today I made it through the door when my mistress went outside. Of course I am not coming back just because they call, "Dinner!" By now I know very well their intentions, so, as usual, I refused. Pasha came to the door inquiring. When my mistress offered him a treat, he looked at her and turned away. After all, Pasha doesn't get to see me very often. Now we are both enjoying ourselves in the yard.

Pasha and Aristotle

I was tied in my yard this morning when suddenly a little black streak flashed into our yard, then jumped on our fence. My mistress called him. He turned his head; she could see his face. Really, he was terrified. He is still a kitten. We heard about Aristotle. He lives three doors away. Pasha has been playing with him for a long time. The family wondered about him. Now my mistress could see what he looked like. He was so frightened that he fell and had to make another try. But the best story is Pasha. He really surprised us. When the kitty fell off the fence, the little fellow couldn't make the jump. Pasha was watching him while he sat on the fence. He followed him with his eyes. He looked concerned. Surely he was not the Pasha we know. Then Pasha followed the little one until he arrived home. Pasha behaved like a father.

Christmas 1982

This is the Christmas season. We are preparing for a visit to our relatives. They have two kitties—the oldest is called Walter. He is part Persian, white, with large black spots all over. He is not friendly and does not want to be held. Maggie is very young, about four months old. She is so sweet—everyone picks her up to love her.

Today is Christmas Eve; at last we are on our way. My mistress is driving, so my master has me on his lap. Today I love him more than ever. I keep kissing and kissing him. This makes my master happy and he thanks me. On the way, I look at my mistress; my master holds me closely so I can't get too close, because I may cause an accident. Just the same, as soon as I could get to her I gave her a big smack on her nose to tell her that I love her too.

When we arrived at the house, we were greeted with holiday joy and excitement. When they saw me looking out of the car, everyone was surprised and looked a little bit hesitant. It wasn't that they did not love me, or were sorry that I came, but they seemed worried about Walter and Maggie. How would they accept me? It would be fun to watch us. They carried me in the house and introduced me to Maggie. Maggie did not approve—that was certain. I went up to say hello to her, but she kept running away from me to hide. As for Walter, he went to pieces. We could all see that I was not approved of. The family decided to put me in a room off the garage. I did not mind in the least. I sat down and looked at Walter. Everyone left me there and closed the door. There is a swinging door big enough for a kitty to go through into his room. The family stood back to observe. I was quite comfortable but Walter was not. He was halfway through the door. All they could see was Walter's behind and his tail going back and forth. Everyone could see that Walter would not accept my friendship.

It was a nice day, so they finally put me outside and tied me to a post. I had a long leash. I enjoyed myself the rest of the day. There were so many birds and bugs to chase. We returned to our motel. I had my comfort box for emergency, and was tied to the bedpost. Later in the evening, I got on the bed to be with my mistress and kept her awake. I decided to bathe myself. This seemed to take all night. My mistress watched me. I never stopped. Around five in the morning I was wide awake, calling them, "It is time for breakfast." They gave me my meal. Still I continued to cry, even after my yeast and vitamins. I went to the back door, which was open just a crack, and pushed myself out. I kept running, with my mistress following me, dressed in her robe. I stopped to do something important, but my mistress was so anxious she grabbed me and I forgot all about it. Back to the motel where I told them in a very loud voice that I was not happy. Loud enough for our neighbors to hear. This could cause a complaint, so my family shoved me in the car and forgot all about me. Later they put me back in the room.

All was quiet for an hour until the family called us to say that they were waiting for us at the office. We were all going out for Christmas brunch. We hurried to leave; then they called, "Cricket, we're leaving." I didn't answer. My family looked all over the room for me. There was not another place to look except for the car, where they searched and I wasn't there. By this time both families were in a panic—they called and called. My master got so upset, and that made my mistress worry more. There was no other place for them to look for me. They all returned to our room. My mistress said that I still had on my leash. At this moment my master saw part of my leash behind the chest drawers. He pulled and pulled. Everone watched him. Then my master pulled out the bottom drawner, where the space under the drawer was less than four inches. I am feeling very comfy, thank you, and looked at them, all in sweet innocence, with no apologies. They picked me up and kissed me, then we all went to breakfast.

My Training

You have heard of the lady from London who trains dogs their bathroom manners. My mistress has been successful with me. It has taken a long time for me to obey her. After all, no one is going to push me around, and I tell her so. I love her so much—more and more, as I grow older, and I try to show her how much. But I go a little too far when she puts me to bed. I especially want to show her how much when I allow her to hold me or fondle me as I rest on the couch. That is too much for me. I can't resist her, so I grab her with my front paws and push my hind feet as hard as I can into her arms. This is painful to her—she is covered with scratches. So when she tries to free herself, she taps my nose or pinches my paws, which hurts horribly. I am a sensitive, delicate kitty, but what else can she do to stop me? So she is on guard every moment she carries me. Now after all this time, she understands that the moment she says no in a stern voice, I get upset and give her more; she can see that flash of anger on my face. Today she understood more. We have a true understanding when I begin. She says, "Good boy, good boy," softly. Now, that's what I like to hear. She can see my expression change just as I remember to stop, which I do. I love to hear her say, "Good boy!" And I really am good. Today my master took me outside for you-know-what. I flatly refused. He used all the magic words, "hurry up," and "quickly," but I just stood there. Then I saw my mistress looking out at me. She said, "Good boy, Cricket," several times.

81

Of course, I would do anything for that, so I quickly made my place. I love the family to tell me I am a good boy.

My Intelligence

My mistress really gets to me. This morning we went out early; you know why. We went through the same old thing. She made two places for me but I was more interested in what was going on—what is in the trees or which kitty is snooping around my playground. So she had to coax me. As usual, I sat down. She thought everything was surely fine, but I got up and covered my empty place. To her amazement I was only pleasing her again. I did not leave anything there.

What can my family do with me? You see, I am very intelligent.

Please Do Not Disturb

We have gone through this before. This morning I was eating my breakfast as fast as I could get it down. My mistress was watching me; then she went to the refrigerator. That did it. I got so excited, I ran with her there. Mabe I thought there was something better coming; but there wasn't, so I returned to my dish. My mistress should know by now that she must not disturb me when I am eating and that I am a sensitive, high-strung kitty. Finally when she understood me; she went to a chair and sat there without saying a word, while I finished breakfast. That's the way I like it and I think she now understands. I love her to be with me when I am eating.

Once More

The family took me shopping with them. Of course, you know what I am going to tell you. Yes, it is about me and my comfort box. Really, the family went into hysterics because I never fail them. So the usual happened. Just as soon as we got started, in my unconcerned way I stepped into my comfort box, which they never foget now. I sat right down as they expected. Now, the car was moving, so they didn't dare to stop because I usually stop too, so they had to drive slowly around the block for me until I was finished. Afterwards I got my usual "Good boy, Cricket," and some pats because I was a good boy and I expected them to tell me so.

My Life

The family loves to have me around them when they are relaxing. Sometimes in the evening they call and call me, but you know I just don't answer them. Yesterday my master called me for almost half an hour. He looked for me in every nook and corner. He became desperate. Soon my mistress was in the act. Both called me. They thought surely I had run away. They called Mama Pearl and Papa Otto for help. Just when they thought I was lost or stolen, my master went into the laundry room again. He looked on the chest of drawers and there I was, sleeping on top of some clean laundry in the basket. Well, I didn't apologize. After all, I have my life to live just the same as they do, and I intend to enjoy myself if I feel like it.

Her Sass

I love to be in the living room when there is no one there, because you know what is fun for me! I am still interested in Persian rugs.

This morning I was there again and about to do my little thing on them with my claws, when my mistress called out sternly, "Stop that! Out, out, Cricket!" You know what I did? I got off the rug, went up on the couch and looked at her straight in her eyes, then dug my claws into the satin cover.

When my mistress gets upset with me, she really tells me so

and I hear her, but finally she is beginning to understand me. By now she knows that I won't take any of her sass and that she must talk softly to me. After all, I am an intelligent kitty; she should know that I will please her if I am in that mood. I was polite about it; I gave her the usual sweet, innocent look, which outright meant no!

Suspicious

After a treat from the table, which was chicken soup, I disappeared to my room. Soon after, my mistress called me. I actually I had my fill, but she called me to dinner loudly. I casually came up the stairs to see what she was going to give me. When I got halfway up, I saw her holding a tablespoon in her hand. That, I knew, must be something icky again, so I stood there looking at her and the spoon. She insisted, so I let her come to me with it. I was surprised when I tasted it and went to lick up the last bit that she dropped on the stairs. Do you know what she gave me? Believe it or not, it was Metamucil.

Run Away

This time my master opened the door to water the garden. He checked with my mistress, who said that I was with her in the den. Soon she forgot about me. She opened the door to get something, then she heard my master say, "Oh-oh, he is out!" This was really too much for them. They were disgusted with me. I didn't care—I already ate my dinner and now I could have fun. They watered the garden thoroughly. Soon I emerged yawning. My master quickly gave me one squirt to get me in, but that was not what I did. Instead I shot across the yard and disappeared again into the darkness. It was 10:00 P.M.—that was the latest that I had ever been away. They left my door open so I could get home and go to bed. Everything was quiet. Then, at 11:30 P.M., my mistress heard a loud sound outside in the distance. (I am scared to death of noise.) Soon she heard another noise—my door! She knew what was coming—ME! As usual, when I run upstairs in a hurry, I missed the curve and fell down, then picked myself up. In a few seconds I came into the bedroom, where the window was wide open. My master was asleep. My mistress was horrified, but she got up and calmly walked to the window, then closed it before I got there.

My Habits

I have been kept indoors because of my weight I gained. It is possible that some kind neighbor may be serving goodies to stray kitties. I don't mind so much; really, my room is comfortable. You know how fastidious I am about my personal habits. Not only my comfort box must be clean, but my whole yard also has to be spaded frequently or I will not oblige the family.

The other day my mistress saw me sniffing suspiciously at the bottom of my comfort box, which was not yet prepared to use. I looked like an anteater—you know how they sniff along without raising their head. My mistress felt embarrassed, so she used Lysol and scoured it with hot water. She was well rewarded, because this morning she was surprised to see both boxes used. On thinking it over, my mistress concluded that I am going just a little bit too far. However, she still scours my comfort boxes each time I use one.

Prince

You would think by now the family should know that I am not interested in meeting any more visitors. Just now my family came home and put my harness on before letting me upstairs. I was all set for my dinner; but who do you think is here visiting us now? His name is Prince. He is part cocker spaniel and most friendly. He is tied up at the end of the hall, wagging and wagging his tail. He is trying hard to be friends with me. His bark is so loud that I growled and hissed at him. Really, this is getting to be too much.

I am not unfriendly. It is just that I am not used to meeting all these strangers. We watched each other from a distance; then we got a little closer. Nothing happened, but you can believe me that I wasn't a friendly host. After a while we did have a little visit together. Of course, I had to stop and talk with him. He really behaved most politely and I did not mind so much. Today the family learned that Prince has moved to another city, so I will never see him again. Now, I wonder: Could we have been good friends? Maybe we could have; he was a good doggie.

Our Relatives

Our relatives Aunt Anna and Uncle Borrie live in London. They are here visiting us. They think that I am the greatest. Of course I am glad to see them when they visit us. I always put on my best manners for them. They came over for a cup of coffee and biscuits. I sat on the floor watching them and never said a word. They bent down to talk with me and remarked on my good manners. I did behave well. After everyone said good-bye and were on their way home, I came into the kitchen and I didn't waste a moment. In a flash I was on the table looking for goodies. I found some butter and as usual helped myself. My mistress couldn't take it all away from me because I had a good bit of it in my tummy. Anyway, she couldn't do a thing about it.

Health Drink

I love to needle my mistress when she comes to me with that health drink. I just look at her, and so it goes each day she pours that stuff into my mouth. Really, by now she must know that I enjoy upsetting her.

Lake Tahoe and Uncle Maurice

Uncle Maurice is an old friend of the family. He is a doctor and comes to our house often. He is so gentle when he holds me that I love him to pet me. Last night, I slept in his room so he could love me more. We got up very early this morning. Uncle Maurice also came over early last night so we could all go to Lake Tahoe. Now we are on our way there. I am all excited and happy. There is lots to see and I tell them about it. We arrived at our cabin. They brought me right in. I am getting used to all this so I didn't seem to be upset. Now that we have been here for two days, I am calming down enough to give them a bad time. Everyone is careful about the front door when they go out. This time they forgot me as they left the cabin. I was the first one to leave, and it was nine o'clock at night. You know what a bad time I gave them before? Well, I did it again. It was pitch dark with only a few lights on. Really it was fun—all three ran after me. This time there were lots of places to hide among the rocks. There were also many cabins close by; I inspected several doorways. By this time Uncle Maurice was getting upset and tired. Then he fell down and said something like, "I broke my ankle." Of course he didn't, but he was really upset that time, and actually very worried that I might run across the road and into the forest where wild animals live. At that moment my master also fell down on his knees. He came up right away. My mistress held her breath. Surely she thought, This is too much—that little brat! They all started out again for me. I darted in and out of the most dangerous places. They kept following me with flashlights. Then when my mistress got close to me, all of a sudden I just allowed her to pick me up. Maybe I was tired of running up and down that hill. My master was not tired, but Uncle Maurice and my mistress felt the high altitude and were ready for bed. They all hugged and kissed me when we got inside. Now do you think that I deserved it? I do, and I just let them love me.

We have been here for five days now. The family noticed that I am feeling listless. Since I had a bladder problem before, they thought I could have it again. I hid in the closet for two days and refused all my food. Uncle Maurice gently picked me up and held me on his lap. He began to tap on my tummy. The family was worried, but Uncle Maurice looked so serious that they had to laugh when he suggested that I could have gas in my tummy. Well, I took that for a few seconds; then I told him, "That is enough!" I growled. They were not quite sure what could be wrong with me, so off we went to see the animal doctor. Uncle Maurice came too. The doctor examined me and gave me some pills to take, which helped. He said that I have bladder trouble. Uncle Maurice is so sweet to me. He watched me carefully. I love him! Do you know what? He thinks I had altitude sickness. No wonder after all that running around we did.

Lake Tahoe: Going Home

We are on our way home. My mistress is driving, but I will not talk to her. This morning she forced some medication in my mouth, which I detest. I just looked at her and walked away. When my master drove, I sat between him and Uncle Maurice. His hands are so gentle. All the way home he fondled me. I enjoyed the ride, but it isn't the same as when we are leaving. Then I get so excited I see everything that is going on and I tell them about it.

Going home, I usually sleep most of the way. When we were nearing home, I jumped up and said, "We are home!" Then I ran as fast as I could into the house as soon as the car stopped.

A Little Bird

My mistress brought me out early this morning. The earth was newly spaded. It was just right for my purpose, so I got down to business. Just as I was in a comfortable position, a little bird flew right up to me, almost in my face, and stood there about a foot away from me for an instant, then he flew away. Of course, I stopped everything to look at him, and that was the end of my business.

The Little Chirper

I must tell you more about my little friend who lives in the treetop. You won't believe it, but it is true. This morning we went outside for the usual morning performance. Just as I was sitting most comfortably, this little chirper called out to me again. We looked to see him standing on a branch, with his little head cocked to the side. He was really giving me the eye. I think he waits for this moment, or maybe he was saying good morning to my mistress. I am not sure; anyway, I didn't budge or look around. I just sat there and stared at him.

Dinner

Whenever we have company for dinner, I always sit in a chair near the table and wait patiently for a little bite. Especially when Uncle John comes to visit us. Somehow he always seems to bring out my best manners without saying a word; he just looks at me and I behave. When I was very young I learned the word *dinner,* and what it means to me. I have given my family a problem. So, they have to spell the word when they speak in front of me.

The other evening we were having a large dinner party. When my mistress called them to sit down, she forgot about me and called *dinner* very clearly. I was in the living room and was ready to eat right then. No one paid any attention to me. They were still talking. As they all came to the table, who should be sitting there on a chair in the center of the table but me. All they could see was my face peering over the table. I was asking, "Where? Where is my dinner?" Still, no one paid any attention to me; but my mistress didn't forget. She picked me up and gave me a little bit of goody from the table.

Same Old Hassle

Every day we go through the same old hassle. My mistress was in the kitchen preparing for guests. She thought surely I would accept my daily vegetable juice; of course, I refused just like that. She said, "Oh, Cricket," as though I might be a little ashamed when she tries so hard to take good care of me. Well, I wasn't; she gave it to me in the patio as usual with a teaspoon, and I swallowed every bit of it. Then I licked my chops and looked at her.

Really, I won't let her get the best of me and she knows it. I gave her the usual innocent expression which outright meant, "No!" Besides, I heard my master giving her the same backtalk about his health drink, but she wouldn't take it from him. I adore it when she asks me to oblige her.

Upset

Sometimes I get so upset with my mistress—she doesn't always pay attention to what I say to her. So today, I really told her.

You see, when I come in for breakfast, I usually go to my dish and eat it, especially if I am hungry. Well, this morning she said, "Eat your breakfast!" There was a little bit left—the vitamins, usually the best part, so she thinks. But I turned away and went to the door. Finally she understood and took me outside, where I did my business. Of course the family was delighted to think that I was house trained, or lets say I trained myself. Anyway, I was proud of myself.

Later the family went out and left me in the patio. When they returned, they saw a catastrophe! The patio was covered with bits of newspaper that I used for my business with some litter green. The family was positively overwhelmed. This time I really told them. They are astounded to think that I am trying so hard to talk to them and they can understand. Of course, I did what I wanted to do.

False Alarm

We have been home for a week since our vacation. Every morning my mistress puts on my harness and ties me outside. I really enjoy my yard. My mistress still puts out my boxes with rugs to keep me warm. I like the one with a cover to keep out the cold wind. I can sit in it and still see everything. It looks like a baby crib. The ground has been spaded and raked for me. This morning my mistress saw me dig a place for myself and I sat down, but nothing happened. So, she made another place for me and I sat in it for a moment. I looked up at her with such sweetness and then walked away. This really concerned the family. Could I have bladder trouble again? Soon after, they brought me to the emergency hospital. When we met the doctor, he looked me over thoroughly and said, "What a healthy kitty." I looked at him in my quiet, regal way. My teeth and gums are beautiful: no tartar. He took out his thermometer. I knew what was coming, so I lay down for the doctor. This surprised him. I had no temperature. The doctor was impressed with me. He said to the family that he enjoyed his work. He has seen many cats, but he said, "Cricket is not a cat. He is too intelligent." Of course, the family was relieved to learn that I am so healthy, and they were proud of my behavior and intelligence.

Our Den

I was outside enjoying myself in the sunshine when I heard an awful commotion. I ran upstairs to see what was happening. There were two men with hammers and other tools making so much noise. It was really pretty messy, with everything scattered around. The men were polite as they worked, but they were not for me. After a while they left, and I took a peek at what happened. Just one look and I disappeared to my room. Soon Mama Pearl and Papa Otto came over to see us. Everyone was sitting in the den and saying how beautiful it looked. My mistress had to get me from downstairs so that I could visit with our company. Well, that is what they thought. Mama Pearl was so sweet. She talked softly, then Papa Otto opened his hand to give me some snacks. I refused that and ran out of the den. No one could understand what happened. I am usually so hungry at any time.

The company stayed for an hour and I still refused to stay;

I even squeezed out of my harness to get away. Well, finally they all got the picture. We have a brand-new rug especially fitted. Everyone remarked how pretty it is, but I don't like it and let them know it. They watched me walk right out of the room.

The Rocking Chair

My mistress was sitting in her rocker; she was busy on the telephone. Just as she completed her conversation, I came up to her smiling, and jumped up on her lap to give her some kisses. Then I lay down on her lap. She was still thinking about some other work to be done, and began to rock me.

That is what I asked for. I snuggled up to her to tell her how happy I was; my face was radiant. You see, she is ususally so busy, and this time I could visit with her. I love her to rock me! I purred and purred. About five minutes later, she put me down so she could complete her work, not realizing how much this meant to me. Well, you know how hurt I was, and I told her so. Then I went to my master in another room and climbed up on his lap; there was no rocker, so he rocked me in his arms. He was so happy to see me. My mistress felt heartsick. I didn't forgive her that evening. Now the family understands, and both of them take time out to rock me every day.

Lots of Fun

With all the love and care my family gives me, you would think by now that my life is running smoothly, but it isn't. You see, since I've been ill, there is nothing for me to do because I am not allowed outside for fear of catching another serious disease. Sometimes I sit on the washing machine and stare outside, wishing and wishing. I do get plenty of sunshine and fresh air. I spend much of my time in the patio. It is a cozy place to stay; I can talk with the family as they pass by and there is always the sun shining here. Pasha misses me very much. He comes to my door and we talk a little. The other day we met at the patio through the glass door. I saw him come in and I put my paw on the glass to greet him. We chatted. One time he got into the house and we kissed before the family could stop us. We can see him walking on the fence; he looks so lonesome. The family always gives him some bits to eat so he won't feel abandoned. Anyway, it isn't really so bad. Hurrah! This was my day. My master got careless and forgot that the door was open. When he came back to go inside, I was there at the door, waiting. I took the advantage; you know how I plan and scheme to get my way. Yes, he was very upset and so was my mistress. They saw Pasha and I kiss, then run off for the afternoon. We had a good time as usual. Later my master called, "Dinner!" and I came running inside. They were surprised to see me come so soon. Well, I do love my home.

Green, Green Grass

Every morning after breakfast, I run to the back door and wait for someone to take me outside for my morning business. Now that it is wintertime and raining, I don't get out so much. Still, I love to eat grass, so I wait for my mistress to cut some for me. She can see me on the washing machine, staring out of the window, calling, "Hurry up!" Usually she cuts the choices ones and brings them to me in a bundle about three inches long. It tastes so good, and I swallow every bit.

But today I asked for a second helping; my mistress returned with another serving. That was just what I wanted; I gobbled it all up.

My mistress is grateful that she can understand me when I talk to her.

Caught

My mistress came into the kitchen. She heard a familiar sound and she was quite right when she got there—I was just helping myself to some milk that was left in the plastic cup. There was really very little, so I had to dig deeply. The cup covered my whole face, so I couldn't see. When she came in I lifted my head; cup and all came with it. What could she say to me? She was laughing. I looked so funny.

My Way

My family thinks that I have expressed myself in many ways. They know how hard I try to make them understand what I am saying. Well, today a lady was visiting us. I had never met her before. They had a snack to eat and, of course, as usual, I asked for my share, so the lady gave me a bite to eat.

Later, when it was close to my dinnertime, I came upstairs to tell the family that it was time to eat. Both my mistress and master were at the end of the hall. I told them over and over that it was dinnertime. They were so enchanted with me that they just stood there and observed me as I pleaded. Of course, they were going to give it to me, my voice was so insistent and pleading. *Really,* they thought. *He is behaving like a child.*

Just then, the lady came into the hall to see what was going on. To their utter amazement, I ran right up to the lady, put my nose on her bare foot, and nudged it. My mistress knew what I was going to do. With that sorrowful expression on my face, I said to the lady, "They won't give me my dinner. Won't you please give me my dinner?" She quickly answered, "Yes, you *can* have your dinner!" With that, my expression changed to joy. I ran into the kitchen, with my proud tail up, as they all followed me. I knew I had won—I was one step ahead of them!

So Happy

The family went away again; this time it was sixteen days. Mama Pearl took good care of me. She brought me green grass every day.

When the family returned, I was so happy to see them, my face lit up. I smiled and smiled at them. When my master picked me up, I gave him four kisses on his nose. I would have given him more, but there was my mistress; she got lots of love too.

Then the first thing I did was run to my comfort box. I showed them what a good boy I was. After that, I never left them. Usually they can never pick me up, but this time I went to my mistress and invited her to pick me up. She did, and I explained to her how good it is to see my family again.

It is a week now since the family came home, and I am still sweeter than ever.

Understanding

This morning the blinds to the living-room windows were closed so I went to my master, looked at him, and then to the closed blinds. He understood. Immediately, he opened the blinds so I could sit and look outside. There is always so much to see.

Shame

It is September now and flea time, so my mistress combed and combed me. She caught several fleas. Of course I am glad to get rid of them, but it becomes boring after a while so I let her know that it was enough. When she didn't stop, I took her arm in my paws, stared at her with a special look of mischief, and grabbed her arm with my paws. My mistress was shocked; she felt the impact of my claws, and it hurt. She hit my paws with the comb and it hurt, but I didn't say a word. Right afterward she brought me to my master and told him about me.

Really, they were positively amazed to see my face. Do you know I was really ashamed? I knew what she was telling him. My expression told them how especially ashamed I felt. I was sitting straight up, my head was bowed, my eyes lowered. The family was touched with such remorse.

95

Rex

My mistress is always snooping around for what she calls script. Surely today she was going to get a great story to tell. Well, it wasn't the great story as expected.

I was in the study, sitting near my master, when what should come into our study but a great big animal! He was so big that my back went up higher than it has ever been. I trembled with fear. My mistress had him by the leash. He is a dog. His name is Rex. Can you imagine her doing a thing like this to me?

Well, my master was here to protect me. He said to my mistress, "Out, out; poor Cricket." He put me on his lap and held me with his arms around me. Our lady friend who brought Rex was right behind my mistress. She was upset with the whole thing, but my mistress wasn't. Perhaps she thought the two of us could be friends. This is great. All will be well. My mistress took the leash from our friend and off he went down the hall, dragging her with him almost to the back stairs. There was a loud thump. When our friend looked out of the study, my mistress was sprawled out, with Rex under her. He was all set to drag her down the stairs, with such enthusiasm no one knew what was coming next.

She picked herself up, feeling a little bit injured someplace. After all, this could be a great experience for both Rex and me, she continued to believe. Down the stairs they both went, my mistress trying to hang on to his leash, our friend following behind to the basement. By this time she was getting nervous.

My mistress suggested that backyard, so out they all went. This will be great, she thought, but it wasn't. Just as they were ready to leave him in the yard, a kitty came by to visit. Of course, that is just what Rex wanted—a kitty to chase. Well, fortunately my mistress still had him by the leash. At that moment he made a leap, and off they started for the kitty. At this time my mistress gave up all hope.

If he stayed downstairs another minute, there would surely be a catastrophe, so back into the house they returned.

They decided to leave him in the tunnel entrance, which is fenced off with a closed gate. This is great, my mistress thought; all is well. Now she will get her script. A few minutes later, our friend went to see her great big baby, who she loves so much. When she looked out, Rex was gone. He had squeezed through the gate bars. "Oh, my! He is gone! He will be run over and killed!" she cried.

My mistress began to panic. They both ran into the street after him. My mistress and her friend cried pathetically, "Rex! Rex!" as they continued to chase him down the street.

A neighbor a few doors away was observing the catastrophe. By this time, Rex was ready to cross the street. He was loving all the excitement. He knew just how to handle his mistress. He was a block away, leaving her in a state of shock.

My mistress was shaking with fear; she continued to race after Rex, then she remembered about the lady who trains dogs, Barbara Woodhouse. She approached Rex calmly and spoke to him as he stopped to visit with a tree. He let her snap on his leash and they both returned to his hysterical mistress.

I Found It

I guess you would think by now that I have learned my lesson, but I haven't. You see, I will always be a naughty kitty. Today my mistress prepared my dinner and put it in the drawer for later. Of course, you know there is nothing that she can do to stop me, and she didn't. I knew that it was my dinner. I tried to get to it, but it was way back in the drawer, but as usual I found a way. There was just a crack, a very small opening, so I took my left paw and brought the dish forward so I could get to it. Then I knew exactly what to do. When my mistress came in, she saw me as I dipped my paw into the dish to scoop up the last bite of dinner. Well, as you might imagine, I did not get any more dinner after that.

Flea Combing

My mistress was going over me with a flea comb and also grooming my fur. I can take so much of that, and then I complain.

Tonight it was so warm, even with the fan on. My mistress was holding me on her lap. She held me with her hands on my back, so I was sitting down facing her, with my tail flashing to and fro. I looked just like a squirrel. Finally I told her again, and stared at her straight into her eyes. I looked at her with such an intense expression. She stared back at me for a long time, observing such intelligence, then smiled at me. With that, I heaved a great big sigh, then I patted her cheek softly. I really meant it, so she carried me off to bed.

The Bribe

The family is most concerned about my personal habits. It is the same old story. I give them such a bad time. Mama Pearl says, "Cricket wants attention," and there is no reason for it when they take me out many times. I positively refuse to perform. I lead my master straight back into the house.

Now they have a good idea. They have decided to bribe me with some goodies. Well, I seemed to catch on quickly because they didn't have to coax me as much. After it is over, they give me the goodies.

Well, now there is another problem. I am so healthy that I can gain weight just eating wood, so my master says. What will they think of next?

Sweet Kitty, or Monster?

Ever since the weather has become sunny and warm, I refuse to use my comfort boxes in the house, so the family has to take me out on my usual jaunts in the yard and coax me with nice words. Today I really don't care that much if my mistress says "Good boy." After all, there is a lot of excitement going on with the birds and other kitties.

Today it was especially nice, so, as usual, I schemed and got through the door when she forgot me. I was gone for two hours.

My mistress thought it useless to call me because I will come when I am good and ready. Later she made some noise on a tin can. I was curious and walked in the house. When she picked me up, I screamed and screeched for her to please leave me alone. The family was shocked. They knew I had gone over to visit Pasha and Socrates. You know how mean Pasha is, and now Socrates is even worse. How could I change so quickly from a sweet kitty to such a monster? I wouldn't allow them to touch me. Later my mistress petted me and pressed on my body to see if I would scream, but I was too sleepy to notice.

The next day we saw our doctor for a checkup. She took my temperature. I lay down nicely for her; she remarked what a good boy I was. After a thorough checkup, she could find nothing wrong with me. When she was finished, I told her what I thought of her. I hissed at her right in the face.

Later, when we returned for my leash, I repeated my insult from across the room. She only smiled.

No one knows what happened. Hereafter the family will be more careful that I don't get out again to associate with naughty kitties.

Mystic

A lady came to our home today; she thinks I am the greatest. She told us all about her kitty, Mystic. Mystic is a one-person cat; he loves her only and is jealous of her husband. One evening when his master was sleeping, believe it or not, Mystic showered him right in the face and he was very wet. Isn't that terrible! Especially since Mystic did it again! Mystic does not want anyone else around his mistress.

The lady also has a rabbit named Gee Gee. Gee Gee is very large. When Mystic comes near him, Gee Gee is careful not to let him tag behind him because Mystic might grab him, but that does not stop him. Mystic looks with glazed eyes at Gee Gee; maybe he would like him for dinner.

Springtime

It is still springtime and there's plenty of green grass around, but not in our yard. All the grass was pulled up to make room for some flowers. Now there is nothing left for me except my special boxes, which were planted just for me. But is doesn't taste the same as the green, green grass that my mistress picked for me. I tried to tell her that I don't like it, but today she came with a bundle again.

Do you know what I did? Really, I was disappointed when she brought it to me again, and I told her so. I stomped on the whole bunch with my paw and pushed it back and forth to show her, then walked away from her. That was really telling her; she understood. Now we have a problem. What can we do about it?

A Frozen Goodie

I was a naughty kitty. Today my mistress heard a loud thump in the kitchen; she came running to see what happened. When she got there, I was ready to open a package of frozen meat. You won't ever guess how I got it from the refrigerator. You see, I learned how to open the freezer while sitting on top of the refrigerator. I was able to push the freezer door open when it was not quite locked. Of course I was disappointed not to eat my frozen goodie, but as you know, I never give up. Later my master was eating his lunch, which smelled so good. He didn't hear me ask him for it, and I couldn't reach the dish, as it was too far away, so I took the place mat in my teeth and pulled it toward me. I almost had the dish when my master looked up from the newspaper he was reading and caught it just in time.

Sandy

The family is up to something again. I am not complaining, but do you know what they are up to now? My mistress is looking for some more script and she insists on getting a puppy for me. She thinks I need company. My master finally agreed.

Believe it or not, when I saw what they were going to bring home to me, I was shocked.

Minnie and Raymond, her son, found a German police dog on a busy highway. Someone had tossed her out. What a dreadful thing to do.

When they brought her home, she was starving. They loved her and named her Sandy. They gave her all the food she could eat, and loving care. She grew fatter and fatter every day. Of course, the family was happy to see Sandy look so well.

A few months later, they were shocked to learn that Sandy was going to be a mother; yes, isn't that something! They quickly made preparations, but were not prepared for more surprises: one puppy, two puppies—"My goodness," they said—three, four, five puppies! *Oh, Dear!* they thought. *What were they* going to do with all these six puppies! OH, THIS WAS IT! No, another puppy! My, my, surely this must be the end! Well . . . Sandy had TWELVE puppies! Of course, the family was delighted, but was feeling a bit numb. What were they going to do with *twelve* puppies?

Minnie and Raymond bought special food for Sandy while she nursed all the puppies. By this time the puppies were eating puppy food. There were six puppies left (the other six were adopted). Every week, Minnie washed two puppies; they looked shining clean and smelled like powder puffs.

When we arrived at the house, I was locked in my carrier in the car, but I could see all the puppies. They were two months old and so full of play. The family stayed a long time, playing with the puppies. Then my mistress picked one up and brought it to the car. Really that puppy was not happy; she cried and cried all the way home and didn't stop crying. When we arrived home, the family put me and my carrier in the bathroom with Penelope and left us alone. I was not in favor of her, and gave Penelope a swat through the bars. Poor puppy; she cried.

Finally the family knew it was useless to try anymore, so my mistress put Penelope in their kingsize bed. My master was so upset; he never did go along with this idea, and now they had to sleep with a puppy. Besides, it was crowded; Penelope weighed twelve pounds.

Finally, my mistress picked Penelope up and lay her on a chair next to her. That is all she wanted, and she fell asleep until the next morning.

Of course, I still refused to talk to Penelope, and she cried when I cracked her again. By the time my master was getting soft, Penelope was lying contendedly on his lap, so he asked my mistress to please remove her. He was getting to love Penelope. Well, this is not the end of my story. The family decided it best to return Penelope to her mother.

When we arrived, all Penelope's brothers and sisters were there. My mistress put Penelope down. To everyone's amazement, all five puppies ran to her and kissed and kissed their little sister on the face. They were so happy to see her again. When my mistress went to speak with the puppies' mother, she glared and growled at her. She said, "You leave my babies alone."

My mistress felt very very sad. She wanted so much to have Penelope, and truly missed her.

Well, you know my mistress. She never gives up.

Of course, the family had to share this story with Uncle Maurice, and he wanted to see all the puppies. When we arrived, he was so overwhelmed with Minnie and her beautiful spirit that he kissed her with gratitude.

A Rainy Day

It is raining all day today, and the family has been waiting for me to do what every kitty should do. They coaxed me with some yeast and milk, which I devoured, and chicken broth which disappeared immediately. I love chicken broth. Still, I have no intention of doing my daily business. Maybe I am enjoying all this attention, especially since I know how concerned they are, so I howled when they locked me in my room with a third container that perhaps I might use.

It is now five o'clock. The family decided to rush me outside before the doctor leaves his office. (They worry about me. You see, it is my bladder problem.) So out my mistress and I went. My master stood in the doorway as the rain started to fall heavily again. Finally my mistress dug in the wet earth a place for me to sit. Surprisingly enough, I sat down. As the rain came down, my mistress held a coat over me so I would not get wet.

After it was all over, we ran into the house. What commotion I caused my family, but I loved it; they even thanked me with "Good boy." Now don't you think I have a loving family?

Paper Bag

The family was busy in the kitchen, so, of course, I was there; one never knows what goodie I can come by. They looked up to see me solemnly walking to the refrigerator, where there are paper bags tucked away against the wall. I stood on my hind legs to reach an available bag. With my claws, I pulled and pulled. They were closely packed. I took one bag down, opened it up, and lay down on it for a nap.

Frightened

I jumped on my master's lap to visit with him; he petted and hugged me. Just as I was falling asleep, my mistress tossed a heavy, yellow-page telephone book on the table near us. I was so frightened that I left my master and ran to another place across the room and stared at the book. My mistress sat at the table and looked at it. I was still frightened, so she removed the book from the room. I was relieved, and ran back to my master's arms. You see, I am a very sensitive kitty.

More Rock-A-Bye

My mistress picked me up to rock me in her arms. She was

sitting on a chair, so she rocked me from side to side in her arms. I tried to tell her that I wanted to be rocked back and forth in the big rocker, but she would not stop, so I jumped out of her arms to my master's lap; he was happy to rock me in the rocker. Later, when my mistress looked up from her book, she saw me and my master sound asleep. He was holding my paw in his hand. We both looked so contented; he had rocked us both to sleep.

Later my mistress picked me up and put me to bed. I said, "Please let me stay," so when she brought me to my room, I ran right back upstairs—something I have never done before—and pushed the door open, but my master was not there; he had gone to bed.

A Ham

The family calls me a ham; they took me to a photographer to have my picture taken. We arrived on a busy, noisy street; I seemd quite calm about it all. My mistress carried me in her arms. I enjoyed it all. As we were walking down the street, three young boys came up to me. They loved me and even kissed me. I reached out my paw to one boy and held his arm. They were so happy to know me and stayed a little while, talking to me. When they went to leave us, I still had the boy's arm in my paw and would not let go. When we arrived at the studio, the photographer brought me in for my picture. Really, I did enjoy myself. When the pictures were developed, I looked so serene and happy, as you can see on the cover of my diary.

I Am a Happy Kitty

It's a long time since I have been outdoors. Really, I miss my adventures with Pasha, so today I slipped out again. No one saw me leave. As usual, I took off for a little spree. Later the family saw me return to my yard. They left me alone just to observe me; so here I am enjoying the afternoon.

My family is quite concerned about my new ways. Ever since my day with Pasha, I have been feeling my oats. This morning my mistress looked out the window. She had a snug box for me with a cover to stop the wind from coming in. It was freezing-cold out, so I stayed there, so warm and comfy. There was another box too for me, with a rug so that I could stay in it when it grew warmer. Just as my family looked out at me, Pasha came by. He walked very politely around me and stood at a comfortable distance. I jumped out of my box and said, "You go away," and he did. My mistress feels upset that I should behave so rudely to my little friend. But, do you know, I think I am growing up! My family has pampered and loved me, so I feel quite secure. I am contented to stay in my yard tied to a post, even if I have to. The birds are chirping and sometimes I believe they are teasing me. My head goes back and forth from one tree to another. I get so excited there is no time to take a nap. Then there are the other kitties who visit me. They usually sit on the fence and stare at me. I growl at them. My family thinks it is strange that I behave so uppity, but that's the way I am. I love my home and my yard. I am a happy kitty.